W9-CDK-494

Little Hands®

SEA LIFE
ART & ACTIVITIES

Creative Learning Experiences for 3- to 7-year-olds

by Judy Press

ILLUSTRATIONS BY MICHAEL KLINE

WILLIAMSON BOOKS W NASHVILLE, TENNESSEE

Library of Congress Cataloging-in-Publication Data

Press, Judy, 1944-
    Little hands sea life art & activities : creative learning experiences for 3- to 7-year-olds / by Judy Press.
        p. cm. – (A Williamson little hands book)
    Summary: Introduces marine animals through the use of crafts, puppets, games, simple experiments, and more.
    ISBN 1-885593-94-5 (pbk.)
    1. Handicraft—Juvenile literature. 2. Marine animals in art—Juvenile literature. [1. Marine animals. 2. Handicraft. 3. Marine animals in art. 4. Scientific recreations.] I. Title: Little hands sea life art and activities. II. Title. III. Series.

TT160.P77798 2004
745.5—dc22

2003060215

Dedication
For Nathaniel,
avec tout mon amour.

Little Hands® series editor: **Susan Williamson**
Project editor: **Emily Stetson**
Interior design: **Linda Williamson, Dawson Design**
Interior illustrations: **Michael Kline**
Cover design and illustrations: **Michael Kline**

Williamson Books
An imprint of Ideals Publications
A division of Guideposts
800-586-2572

10 9 8 7 6 5 4 3 2 1

Acknowledgments
I wish to thank the following people for their support and encouragement in the writing of this book: the Mt. Lebanon Public Library and its children's librarians; the South Hills writers' group; my talented friends Carol Baicker-McKee and Andrea Perry; my husband, Allan; my children, Brian Joseph and Aliza, Debbie and Mark, Darren and Lara, and Matt; and my cherished grandchildren, Anaelle and Nathaniel.
    This book would not have been possible without the talent and dedication of the following people at Williamson Books: Susan and Jack Williamson, Dana Pierson, Emily Stetson, Jean Silveira, Vicky Congdon, and Sarah Rakitin. A special thanks to designer Linda Williamson and illustrator Michael Kline for their creative talents.

CONTENTS

Welcome to the Sea!   4

A Message to Grown-Ups   5

Who Lives in the Sea?   6
Sea-Life Mobile   7
Bony Fish Skeleton   10
Shark   14
My Aquarium   18

Amazing Fish, Funny Fish   22
Reef Fish   23
Amazon Leaf Fish   27
Flat Flounder   29
Sea Horse   32
Porcupine Fish   36

The Sandy Shore   38
Sand Dollar   39
Scallop   41
Black Oystercatcher   44
Crab Pincers   46
Manatee   48

In the Tide Pool   51
Tide Scene   52
Sea Urchin   55
Hermit Crab   57
Sea Star   60

The Coral Reef   64
Colorful Coral   65
Sea Anemone   68
Angelfish   70
Giant Clam   72
Lettuce Sea Slug   75

The Kelp Forest   77
Giant Kelp   78
Sea Otter   82
Brown Turban Snail   85
Garibaldi Fish   87

The Open Sea   90
Jellyfish (Sea Jelly)   91
Sea Turtle   94
Sailfish   98
Dolphin   101

In the Deep   104
Lantern Fish   105
Octopus   107
Giant Squid   110

The Polar Sea   113
Seal   114
Adélie Penguin   117
Blue Whale   120
Krill   124

Index with Activity   126
List by Skill Level

WELCOME TO THE SEA!

Many creatures live in the sea.
Let's find out who they might be!
In this book we will explore
From beaches to the ocean floor.

There are fish with bones (and some without)
That like to swim and dart about.
Some fish have jaws that open wide,
So smaller fish get caught inside.

Hiding at the sandy shore
Are shells and birds and so much more.
Critters with pincers scuttle along,
Hurrying to get where they belong.

Where forests of kelp drift and sway,
Schools of fish swim, hide, and play.
And sea otters munch afternoon snacks
While floating lazily on their backs.

Colorful fish come and go
Where the coral gardens grow.
But in the deep it's dark as night,
So clever fish turn on a light!

The water's cold farther away,
In the places penguins stay.
Elsewhere in the chilly seas,
Seals swim fast and playfully!

So even if the ocean's far from you
In your play you can go there too,
Turn the page and look inside,
This sea-life book will be your guide!

A MESSAGE TO GROWN-UPS

Young children delight in discovering the surprises and secrets of our incredible watery world — even if they have never actually stood on its shores. Through hands-on crafts and activities that are easy to do at home or school, *Little Hands® Sea Life Art & Activities* introduces children anywhere to the wondrous creatures and plants that make their homes in or near the sea — NO BEACH IS NEEDED!

As children explore seven different ocean habitats, they discover how each plant and animal is the same as or different from all others and how it is specifically adapted to its watery world. Each craft includes extended activities that enrich the experience while teaching early learning skills: observation, compare and contrast, shape recognition, counting, language development, and fine and gross motor development. Plus, there are ample opportunities for creative expression and imaginative play through open-ended art, fingerplays, action poems, pretend play, and games.

Ocean Art & Crafts

While each of the age-appropriate crafts includes easy-to-follow instructions, the intent is that children will make personal choices and follow their own muses. Avoid holding up perfectly completed projects as examples, as they tend to intimidate the young crafter and stifle creativity. Encourage new ideas, fanciful designs, and individual interpretations so that each piece of art reflects the child who made it.

The fish symbol next to each craft indicates the relative skill level involved in each project. Three fish indicate a more challenging activity; one fish identifies the easiest projects.

Small Fry Fun suggestions are provided for simpler adaptations geared to younger crafters or less advanced beginners.

Craft Fun & Safety

For any craft activity, always remember to work in a well-ventilated room and choose and control materials according to your young crafters' propensity to put small objects into their mouths. Paper fasteners and paper clips, for example, can present choking and poking hazards. Remember, too, that younger siblings may pick up odds and ends from the floor or pull items off the table's edge. Make sure all cleanup is thorough. Always supervise water play: Even small amounts of water may pose a drowning risk. Likewise, baking or the use of any sharp or pointed object should be done only by an adult. Young children should only use child safety scissors.

Share in the Fun!

Most important, maintain a relaxed, fun, and lively atmosphere where a good time can be shared by all. *Little Hands® Sea Life Art & Activities* is written for children and the grown-ups in their lives. Use this time together to share in the joy of creating and the excitement of learning! Share stories of real and imaginary ocean experiences. Talk about "what if?" and "can you imagine?" Keeping the conversation going as kids work on their art and crafts enhances the learning and gives children an opportunity to share their thoughts.

So, whether the real ocean is close by or far away; whether a visit to the beach is a pleasant memory or just a dream, dive in! The wonders of the ocean are waiting for you!

WHO LIVES IN THE SEA?

Can you name some things that might live in the ocean? Yes, **FISH** of all shapes, sizes, and colors live there. And you're right if you said **PLANTS**, like seaweed, live in the sea, too. You can see seaweed when it washes up on shore, or when it waves like a field of grass above the shallow water and in the salt marshes.

But fish and plants are not all that live in the sea. There are also playful **DOLPHINS**, swift **SEA TURTLES**, and jiggly **JELLYFISH**. You can have noisy **SEABIRDS** at the seashore, too. And don't forget the eight-armed **OCTOPUS** and the biggest animal of all: the **WHALE**! They are all part of sea life.

The ocean is a wonderful place, home to many different kinds of sea plants and sea creatures. "Dive in" to the wonders of the ocean and get to know them better!

MANY CREATURES LIVE IN THE SEA,
THEY SWIM AND DIVE AND CRAWL.
THEY'RE ROUND AND FLAT AND STRIPED AND PLAIN,
THEY'RE BIG AND FAT AND SMALL!

Sea-Life Mobile

What you need

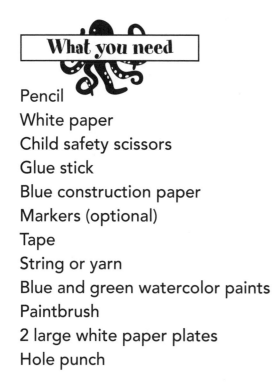

Pencil

White paper

Child safety scissors

Glue stick

Blue construction paper

Markers (optional)

Tape

String or yarn

Blue and green watercolor paints

Paintbrush

2 large white paper plates

Hole punch

WHAT YOU DO

1 Draw sea creatures (or trace them from a book) onto white paper and cut them out. Name each creature as you cut it out.

2 Glue the creatures onto blue construction paper. Cut them out. Decorate with markers if you like. Tape string to the back of each one.

3 Paint the front and back of one paper plate to look like the sea. Let dry. Punch three holes around the rim. Thread string through the holes to hang the mobile.

Glue plates together

4 Ask a grown-up to cut out the center of the other paper plate. Tape the strings to the inside rim of the plate. Glue the plates together.

• •

small fry FUN

Draw and color different sea creatures on a sheet of paper.

Sea-Life Matchups

Have a grown-up help you cut out an even number (2, 4, 6, or 8 is an *even* number) of white paper squares. Draw the same sea creatures or plants on pairs (two) of squares. Draw as many pairs of different sea creatures or plants as you want. (You can find lots of pictures in this book to copy.)

To play, turn the squares over so the pictures don't show. Mix them up. Pick up one card and call out the name of the sea creature or plant. Turn over another card and name *that* animal or plant. If the pictures match, put the cards aside in a pile. If not, turn both cards back over and try matching again. If playing with others, take turns until all the matches are found.

SAME OR DIFFERENT?

Lots of living things share a home at the ocean. And each living thing is very different from the others! Look at the pictures on page 6 again, and then play *Same or Different?*

What is the SAME about sea life?

They live in or near the sea, spending time in or near the water.

They need salt water instead of fresh (unsalty) water.

They swim or float or grow in water, or fly over it, looking for food!

What is DIFFERENT about sea life?

Some are plants and others are animals.

Some live in the water, some on land, and some in both places.

Some come up for air and others "breathe" underwater.

Some have bony skeletons and others don't.

Some have shells on the outside and some have scales.

Some lay eggs and others have babies.

Can you name one example of each?

A Swim through the Sea BY KRISTIN JOY PRATT

In the Swim BY DOUGLAS FLORIAN

Somewhere in the Ocean BY JENNIFER WARD AND T. J. MARSH

Bony Fish Skeleton

THERE ARE MANY DIFFERENT FISH SWIMMING IN THE SEA. MOST HAVE LOTS OF BONES INSIDE, JUST LIKE YOU AND ME!

What you need

Child safety scissors
White paper plate
Glue
Black construction paper
Flat toothpicks

WHAT YOU DO

1 Cut out the fish's head, fins, and tail fin from the paper plate. Glue onto the construction paper.

2 Break toothpicks into different-sized pieces. Glue onto the paper for fish bones.

small fry FUN

Draw a fish skeleton on black paper using white chalk or a crayon.

Back to Back

*B*ony *fish*, like salmon and trout, have backbones made up of separate pieces of bone called *vertebrae*. (Those bones are why you have to be so careful when you eat them!) And guess what? You have vertebrae, too!

Sit on the floor back to back with a partner. Raise your knees, but keep your feet on the floor. Now, try to stand up without using your hands. You and your friend help keep each other up, similar to how your backbone supports you when you're standing on your own!

Question & Answer

MY MOM SAYS I'M A FISH WHEN I SWIM, BUT I'M *NOT* REALLY A FISH, AM I?

Of course not! And not everything that swims in the ocean with *fins* — the parts of a sea creature's body that stick out on the sides, top, or bottom — is a fish, either. (It takes more than that to be a fish, you see.) Fish also have slit-like openings called *gills* to get oxygen from the water. All fish are *cold-blooded* — the temperature of their bodies changes to match the temperature of the water or air around them. Most fish have *scales* (hard plate-like pieces on their skin) too. And, like you, fish have some kind of *backbone* (an inner skeleton). Some fish also have a *swim bladder,* which works sort of like a built-in life preserver, to help them float.

So, even if you're swimming in the ocean, *you* can't be a fish! You have no fins growing on your body, no gills (you breathe oxygen from the air, not from the water like a fish!), or scales, and your body stays nice and warm — 98.6°F (37°C) — no matter what the water temperature is!

About Fish: A Guide for Children BY CATHRYN SILL

REST TIME!

Fish don't sleep the way people do,
with their eyes closed,
but they do have busy times and resting times.
Some fish, like the *nurse shark,*
rest on the ocean floor without moving.
Some other fish must keep moving even when they rest, in order to breathe.

LOOK FOR A QUIET PLACE TO REST.
Add a soft pillow, a favorite toy, and a picture book.
You may even fall asleep!

IF I WERE A GREAT BIG FISH

You can't really be a fish, but you can pretend to be one, using your whole body!

If I were a great big fish,
(open arms wide)
I could swim all day.
(move arms behind body, like a fin)
There'd be lots of other fish
(wiggle fingers)
With whom I could play.
(wiggle fingers together)
I'd dive down to the ocean floor
(place hands together in diving motion)
And take a look around.
(look both ways)
Then I'd swim back up again
(paddle hands up)
And I'd dive right back down.
(paddle hands down)
When I got too tired,
(rub eyes)
I'd coast with the tide,
(hands behind head)
And take a little nap,
(put head down on arm)
With my eyes open wide!
(open eyes wide)

Shark

SOMETIMES JUST THE SIGHT OF SHARKS GIVES PEOPLE QUITE A FRIGHT. ALTHOUGH THEY LOOK SO SCARY, MOST DON'T EVEN BITE!

What you need

Child safety scissors
2 sheets of construction paper
Tape
Small white paper plate
Glue
Wiggly eyes (optional)
Black marker

WHAT YOU DO

1 Cut one sheet of construction paper into a square (see page 73, step 1). Overlap the corners and roll into a cone. Tape to hold.

2 Ask a grown-up to cut out the shark's upper and lower jaws full of teeth from the center of the paper plate. Trim the outside edge of the plate to fit the opening in the cone. Tape in place.

3 Cut out the shark's fins from the second sheet of construction paper. Bend back the ends for tabs. Tape the tabs onto the shark.

4 Cut out the shark's tail and tape it to the end of the cone. Glue on the wiggly eyes. Draw the shark's gill slits.

● ●

small fry **FUN**

Use a pen to draw a shark onto a plastic-foam tray (from fruits or vegetables only). Cut out the shark. Float it in a tub or sink of water.

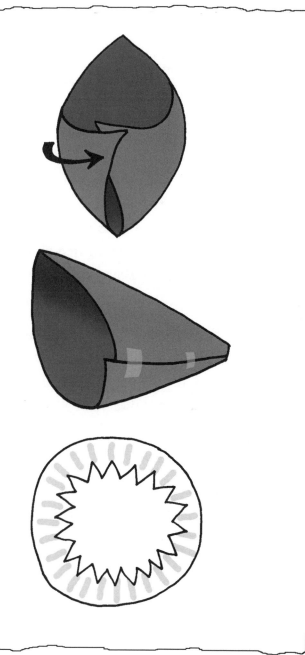

SPECTACULAR SHARKS!

WHY SHARKS ARE SPECIAL FISH

Sharks are different from other types of fish (page 11). Their skeletons are made of flexible *cartilage.* (You have cartilage in your earlobes!) There's another difference too: Sharks don't have a *swim bladder* to help them float (page 12). To keep from sinking to the bottom of the sea, sharks use oil! The oil in a shark's liver is lighter than the water.

TRY IT: Fill a glass with water; drip vegetable oil on top. Does the oil sink or float?

SHARP SHARK TEETH!

Sharks have many rows of sharp teeth with jagged edges, like a saw with lots of blades. When a shark loses a tooth, or when a tooth is broken, a new one moves forward from the row behind it. A shark uses up *thousands* of teeth every year!

TRY IT: How many rows of teeth do you have in your mouth? What happens when you lose a baby tooth? Does a new tooth replace your lost tooth?

SUPER SMELLER

A shark's sense of smell is so powerful that it can smell things in the water many feet (cm) away.

TRY IT: Gather several things that have strong scents, such as cinnamon, garlic, and a slice of lemon. Close your eyes and see if you can identify each scent. Name something you like to smell. What *don't* you like to smell?

I'M SCARED OF SHARKS! DON'T SHARKS BITE PEOPLE?

Some types of sharks, such as the great white, sometimes attack people, but most sharks are not dangerous. In fact, most sharks aren't interested in people at all! Still, the best place to see a shark up close is at an aquarium, where there's protective glass between you and the shark. It's very exciting to watch it cruise around the tank!

LITTLE HANDS STORY CORNER™

Sharkabet: A Sea of Sharks from A to Z BY RAY TROLL

My Aquarium

THERE ARE FISH IN MY AQUARIUM,
I FEED THEM EVERY DAY.
THEY CAN TRAVEL BACK AND FORTH,
BUT THEY CANNOT SWIM AWAY!

What you need

Child safety scissors
Blue construction paper and scraps
 of assorted colors
Clear contact paper
Glue
Black marker

WHAT YOU DO

1 Cut out fish and seaweed from the paper scraps. Press them between two pieces of clear contact paper.

2 Cut border strips from the blue paper. Glue them to the edges of the contact paper to frame your aquarium scene.

small fry **FUN**

Ask a grown-up to cut a small window in the center of a paper plate. Cut slits as wide as the window on both sides of the plate. Draw fish on a long strip of cardboard. Pass the strip of cardboard through the slits to see the fish swimming across the window.

AT THE AQUARIUM

Everything that swims, crawls, flies, or grows lives in a special home, or *habitat*, that's just right for it. At the ocean, one animal's habitat may be at the bottom of the sea, while skimming along the water's surface might be the perfect home for another creature.

An *aquarium* is a man-made home for animals and plants that live in or around water. Scientists re-create the natural habitats of the animals, matching the temperature of the water and the light as closely as possible. You can see creatures of the deep in tanks that have special lights. You can see fish swimming so close that only the glass and a little water separate you from them! There may even be exhibits that allow you to actually touch — very carefully, of course! — the creatures that live there, such as the sea urchins and sand dollars in a tide pool (pages 51 to 63). The aquarium is a fascinating place!

If you don't have an aquarium near your home, you can visit one online.

www.mbayaq.org (Monterey Bay Aquarium)
www.sheddnet.org/ (John G. Shedd Aquarium)
www.aqua.org/ (National Aquarium in Baltimore)

Make an Edible Aquarium!

Ask a grown-up to prepare a box of blue gelatin dessert. Pour it into a clear bowl or cup. Refrigerate for one hour. Add gummy fish to the mixture and rechill until firm. Enjoy!

HABITATS ARE HOMES!

GO ON A HABITAT HUNT!

A habitat is where a plant or animal can find just the right food, shelter, and water. Different creatures can share the same habitat.

TRY IT: Look for plants and animals that live in habitats near you. Can you find any insects, birds, or other animals living in trees, bushes, or on the ground outside? Draw a picture of different habitats you see and the creatures that live there. Now draw a picture of the habitat *you* live in!

CREATE A PRETEND AQUARIUM

TRY IT: Gather several large empty cereal boxes. Ask a grown-up to cut an opening in the front of each box. Draw sea-life creatures on paper and cut them out. Hang the cutouts from strings taped inside the box. Make a separate "exhibit" for the coral reef, the polar seas, the deep sea, the shore, the tide pool, and other ocean habitats you'll find in this book.

My Visit to the Aquarium
BY ALIKI

AMAZING FISH,
FUNNY FISH

Some fish come in many colors,
They're yellow, blue, and green.
Others hide in a disguise,
Hoping they won't be seen!

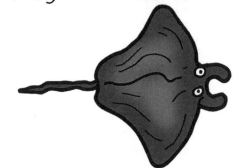

REEF FISH MUST BE VERY SMART,
THEY KNOW HOW TO FOLLOW RULES.
THEY SWIM AWAY FROM LARGER FISH,
AND TRAVEL BACK AND FORTH IN SCHOOLS!

Reef Fish

What you need

Child safety scissors

White paper plates

Watercolor paint

Paintbrush

Markers

Glue

Wiggly eyes (optional)

Paint stirrers or craft sticks

WHAT YOU DO

1 Cut fish from the paper plates. Paint with watercolors. Let dry.

2 Draw the fishes' mouths and scales. Draw eyes or glue on wiggly eyes.

3 Glue fish onto the sticks. Act out a made-up puppet play using your different fish!

. . . .

Cut out fish from different-colored paper, including one from blue paper. Glue onto a large sheet of blue paper. Decorate with markers or crayons if you like. Is it hard to find the blue fish on the blue water?

FISH SCHOOL!

Have you watched fish swim in an aquarium or fish tank? Often the same kind of fish swim together in a group called a *school*. Each fish watches the other fish around it and then moves in the same direction and at the same speed. When one turns, the others turn, as if they're in a dance. In the sea, blending in with the crowd means there's less of a chance that you'll be noticed by a bigger fish and get eaten!

FISH SCHOOL ART

TRY IT: Ask a grown-up to cut out a fish shape from a sponge. Pour a small amount of tempera paint into a dish or lid. Dab the sponge into the paint and press several fish onto paper, all going in the *same* direction. Then press a fish shape going in the *opposite* direction. Which fish do you notice first?

MAKE UP A FISH DANCE

TRY IT: Standing with a group of friends, one person begins a motion, such as waving his arms or tapping his feet, and the others follow. Then another person does a different motion, and everyone switches again. Keep your eyes on everyone else so you all stay together — just like a school of fish!

Question & Answer

DO FISH TALK IN SCHOOL?

Could you go to school without talking? No way? Well, fish "talk" also — sort of. They make sounds by rubbing their teeth together or vibrating their swim bladders (page 12).

Hear the hum. Thread a long piece of strong yarn through two holes in a large button. Tie the ends of the yarn together. Pull the yarn so that you have a few inches (cm) on each side of the button. Loop your fingers through the yarn and twirl the button around. Now pull the twisted string in and out. The button will twirl, and you'll hear a humming sound as the string vibrates!

Little Hands Story Corner™

Fish Wish BY BOB BARNER

One Fish Two Fish Red Fish Blue Fish BY DR. SEUSS

SOME FISH ARE VERY SNEAKY,
THEY'RE MASTERS OF DISGUISE.
BLENDING IN WITH THEIR SURROUNDINGS,
THEY'RE HARD TO RECOGNIZE!

Amazon Leaf Fish

What you need

Paintbrushes

Orange, brown, red, and green tempera paints, in dishes or lids

Large leaf with rounded edges and a stem

Blue construction paper

Marker

WHAT YOU DO

1 Brush the orange, brown, and red paint onto the leaf.

2 Turn the leaf paint-side down on the blue paper. Rub over the back of the leaf to make a print. Remove the leaf; let the paint dry. Draw the leaf fish's mouth, eye, gill, fins, and tail fin.

3 Paint undersea plants and sea life around the fish.

Question & Answer

IS A *LEAF FISH* AN ANIMAL (LIKE A FISH) OR A PLANT (LIKE A LEAF)?

Good question! A leaf fish is a fish, but it is disguised so well that it *looks* like a plant leaf! The leaf fish lives in muddy water surrounded by real leaves. It's an expert at *camouflage* — hiding from its enemies by disguising itself or blending in with its surroundings. Animals in the sea and on land use camouflage all the time. Can you think of another one?

LEAF FISH FUN!

PRETEND PLAY!

It's fun to pretend to be someone or something else! What is your favorite disguise — a funny clown, a princess, or a fierce lion?

TRY IT: Put on a disguise. Did you surprise anyone?

PAPER PICK-UP

Have a grown-up tear red and green paper into an equal number of small pieces. Scatter the paper onto green grass. Pick up the paper pieces as quickly as you can (have a grown-up time you). After three minutes, count how many red and green squares you picked up. Which was easier to find, the green or the red paper?

Flat Flounder

ON THE SANDY SEAFLOOR,
THE FLOUNDER LIKES TO HIDE.
HERE'S WHAT'S SO AMAZING:
BOTH EYES ARE ON ONE SIDE!

What you need

Old newspaper
2 brown paper lunch bags
Tape
Child safety scissors
Brown marker

WHAT YOU DO

1 Fold a sheet of newspaper so it can fit inside one bag.

2 Place the bag with the bottom flap facing down. Fold under the four corners. Tape to hold.

3 Cut the fish's tail fin and fins from the second paper bag. Tape onto the fish. Draw the fish's eyes, gills, and spots.

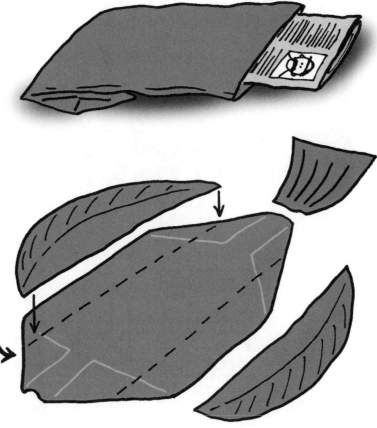

fold under these corners →

• •

small fry FUN

Flatten a ball of Play Clay (page 55) into a pancake. Use a plastic knife to cut out a flat fish. With a pencil, poke two eyes and a mouth.

LittLe HANDS STORY CORNER™

Swimmy
BY LEO LIONNI

WHY IS A FLOUNDER FLAT?

Being flat is a good thing if you're swimming on the seafloor the way the flounder does, trying not to be seen. As the flounder grows, its body flattens and turns, until it lies on its side with both eyes on the top side — perfect for looking up!

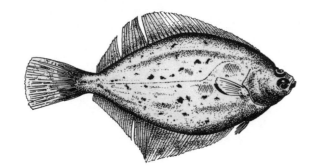

FLOUNDER FUN!

MY, HOW YOU'VE GROWN!

Look at your baby pictures. Compare them to the way you look today. How have *you* grown and changed?

PLAY FLOUNDER HIDE AND SEEK!

Hide, lying down flat like a flounder in whatever spot you choose. See if an "enemy fish" can find you. Can you hide as well as a flounder can? Do you have to move your head to see other fish?

I'm a Sea Horse

Here are things about a sea horse
You may want to know.
It doesn't neigh or shake its head,
("Neigh" and shake head)
Or stop when it hears, "Whoa!"
(walk, then stop)
A sea horse can't march in a parade,
(do marching steps)
Or shake its long brown mane.
(shake head back and forth)
It doesn't eat a bucket of oats,
(lower head and pretend to eat)
Or gallop 'cross a plain.
(take galloping steps)
But a sea horse does have dorsal fins
(flutter hands like fins)
And lives out in the sea.
(look out with hand to forehead)
It hides among the sea grass
(hide behind fingers)
And swims so gracefully!
(swimming motion)

Sea Horse Scene

What you need

Child safety scissors (wavy-edged
scissors optional)
Small white paper plate
Black marker
Green and blue construction paper
Glue
Small seashells (optional)

WHAT YOU DO

1 Cut out sea horse shapes from the
   edge of the paper plate.

2 Draw the sea horses' eyes and
   armored plates.

3 Tear seaweed shapes from the green paper.
   Glue them onto the blue paper. Glue the sea
   horses on top.

4 Draw other fish swimming. Draw or glue small
   seashells on the bottom of the picture.

small fry
FUN

Draw S shapes onto paper.
Add eyes and a long jaw to
each S to make a sea horse.
Color sea grass for your sea
horses to hide in!

Question & Answer

> **IF A SEA HORSE IS A FISH, WHY IS IT CALLED A HORSE?**

Look at the picture of a sea horse and the picture of a real horse. Do they look alike in any way? You may notice one thing in common — a long *snout*. That's where the tip of the nose is. (On a horse, this part of the body is called a *muzzle*.)

Though a sea horse looks like a horse in some ways, it has gills and fins — just like other fish!

One Lonely Sea Horse
BY SAXTON FREYMANN

HORSING AROUND!

MIND YOUR TABLE MANNERS!

Sea horses are very noisy eaters! They have no teeth, so they swallow their food whole, sucking up entire shrimp!

TRY IT: Use a straw to suck up a small amount of milk in a glass. What sound do you make? How about the sound when you suck in spaghetti between your lips?

GUESS WHO?

The sea horse moves through the water with its head *up* and its tail *down*. What other animal swims along with its head up and tail down when it's in the water? (Hint: It does the doggie paddle!)

BEAUTIFUL ANIMALS

A lot of people love to watch horses, and some people learn to ride them. The sea horse is also beautiful to watch, but can be very shy. You may have to look close to see it!

TRY IT: Go to a pet store or aquarium and watch the sea horses. Does the sea horse gallop or rock? Does it pound the water or float gently along? Does it look heavy or light? What *describing* words would you use for a sea horse?

Porcupine Fish

WHEN THIS FISH GETS ANGRY,
IT LOOKS LIKE A PORCUPINE.
IT PUFFS ITSELF INTO A BALL
THAT'S COVERED WITH SHARP SPINES!

What you need

Child safety scissors
Construction paper scraps
Glue
Pinecone
Wiggly eyes

WHAT YOU DO

1 Cut out the porcupine fish's mouth, fins, and tail fin from construction paper. Glue onto the pinecone.

2 Glue on wiggly eyes.

Question & Answer

HOW DOES A PORCUPINE FISH GET SO ROUND AND PRICKLY?

When danger appears, the porcupine fish pumps water into special sacs until its spiny body balloons up into a prickly ball. It makes itself so big and prickly that it's not easy (or yummy) for another fish to swallow it. Being prickly is the porcupine fish's defense against being eaten!

PRICKLY FISH FUN

PLAY PRICKLY CATCH

Toss a smooth ball back and forth to a friend. Then gently toss a prickly hairbrush back and forth (keep it low, away from your head!). Which is easier to catch? Imagine if the hairbrush were covered with pointy spines! Ouch!

THE SANDY SHORE

Walking on the sandy shore,
There's so much there to see —
Crabs, shells, busy seabirds,
And castles by the sea!

Sand Dollar Rubbing

YOU CAN'T USE THESE FOR MONEY. (THEY'RE NOT EVEN WORTH A BUCK.) BUT IF YOU FIND ONE ON THE SHORE, IT MIGHT BRING YOU GOOD LUCK!

What you need

Child safety scissors
Plastic-foam tray (from fruits or vegetables only)
Dull pencil
White paper
Crayon

WHAT YOU DO

1 Cut out a circle from the center of the plastic-foam tray.

2 Use the pencil to press a five-petal pattern in the center of the foam sand dollar.

3 Place the paper on top of the foam sand dollar with the raised petal pattern facing up. Rub back and forth with the crayon. Lift the paper to see your sand dollar rubbing!

FUNNY FEET

Sand dollars belong to a group of "spiny-skinned" animals that aren't fish.
They don't swim with fins, but they have a very interesting way to get around and eat.
They use the tube-like feet on the undersides of their bodies to gather food as they move slowly through the sand!

Beach Day
BY KAREN ROOSA

Stella, Star of the Sea
BY MARIE-LOUISE GAY

Scallop Shell

Pink construction paper
Child safety scissors
Crayons
Black marker
Glue
Cotton balls

BE A SCALLOP

Scallops move through the water,
(swim one hand through air in front of you)
Propelled just like a jet.
(zoom other hand fast the other way)
They clap their shells together,
(clap hands)
Just like a castanet!
(hands out, fingers to thumb,
like playing castanets)

WHAT YOU DO

1 Fold the pink construction paper in half. Cut out a scallop shell, leaving the "foot" of the shell at the folded edge as shown.

foot

2 Color the outsides of the shells with two different colors. Add stripes for ridges. Use the black marker to draw the "eyes" of the scallop inside the shell.

3 Glue cotton balls inside the shell halves for the soft body of the scallop.

Question & Answer

AREN'T SCALLOPS THE SEAFOOD FROM THE STORE? THESE SHELLS DON'T LOOK LIKE WHAT WE HAVE FOR DINNER!

A scallop is one of the shelled sea creatures known as *mollusks* (not fish). But you're right — when you buy scallops in a store, they don't have their shells. On the seafloor, scallops live in their shells, filtering food from the water. At the beach you can find empty scallop shells — some pink, gray, orange, white — that have been pushed in by the waves.

SHELL FUN

"HI, BI!"

How many matching parts does a scallop shell have? Let's count them — one, two. A scallop has *two* halves to its shell, so it's called a *bivalve*. The "bi" means "two"! How many wheels does a bicycle have? Two again!

TRY IT: Think of other things that come in twos or in matching pairs. What about a salt and pepper shaker? Now you name one!

FEEL THE RIDGES ...

Fold a sheet of paper back and forth like a fan. Open the paper. Close your eyes and feel the ridges. Many scallops have deep ridges on their shells too.

... FEEL THE FORCE

To move quickly, scallops clap their shells together, forcing water out from between the shells, which pushes the scallops forward.

TRY IT: Clap your hands together under water. Do you feel the water move?

START A COLLECTION!

It's lots of fun to collect colorful shells and stones. Wash them off, then sort them by colors or shapes or sizes. Display them on a shelf or in a pretty dish. (But please, never, ever take a shell that has a living creature inside. The animal will die, and the shell will smell like rotten fish! Yuck!)

Black Oystercatcher

LISTEN TO THE OYSTERCATCHER,
WITH ITS NOISY SHRIEK.
IT CAN OPEN UP A SHELL
WTH ITS POINTY BEAK!

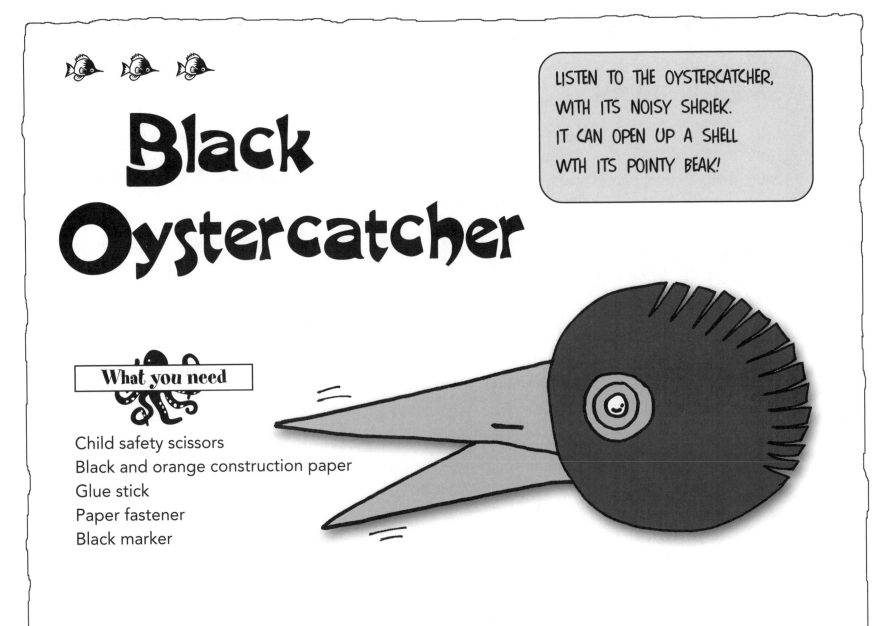

What you need

Child safety scissors
Black and orange construction paper
Glue stick
Paper fastener
Black marker

WHAT YOU DO

1 Cut out a circle of black construction paper. Cut fringe along one side of the circle.

2 Cut out two halves of the bird's beak from the orange paper. Cut out a small orange circle and glue it onto the black circle for the bird's eye.

3 Ask a grown-up to poke the paper fastener through the center of the small orange circle and both halves of the beak as shown.

4 Use the black marker to draw a nostril on the beak and a black circle around the paper fastener as shown on finished bird.

Bird Talk

Oystercatchers are noisy birds! While guarding their eggs or young, they will scurry alongside an approaching person, scolding them with a harsh piping call!

Go on a nature walk with a grown-up. Listen to the different birdcalls. Try to repeat each call. Did you fool any birds into thinking you were one of them?

Crab Pincers

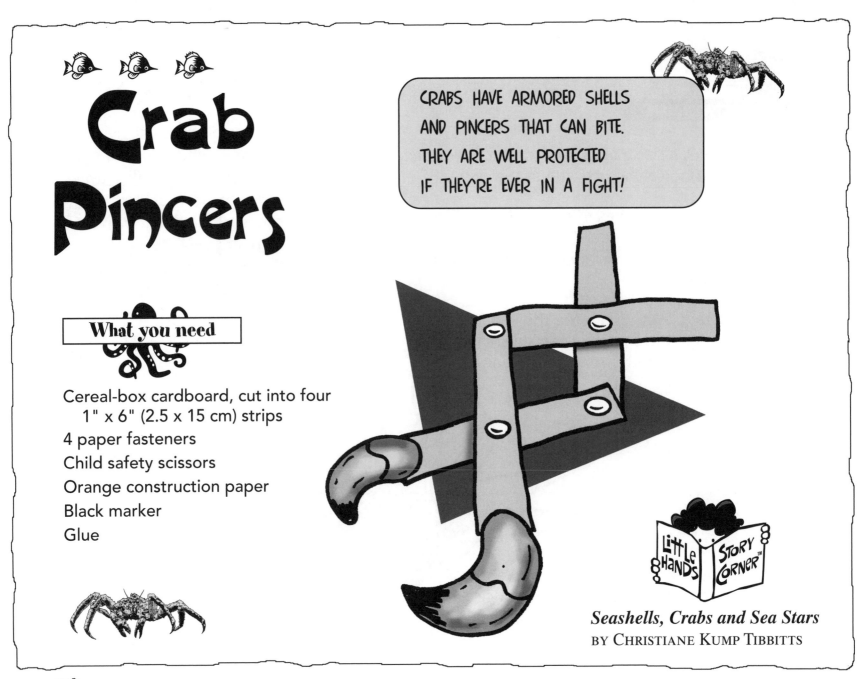

CRABS HAVE ARMORED SHELLS AND PINCERS THAT CAN BITE. THEY ARE WELL PROTECTED IF THEY'RE EVER IN A FIGHT!

What you need

Cereal-box cardboard, cut into four 1" x 6" (2.5 x 15 cm) strips

4 paper fasteners

Child safety scissors

Orange construction paper

Black marker

Glue

Seashells, Crabs and Sea Stars
by Christiane Kump Tibbitts

WHAT YOU DO

1 Make an X with each pair of cardboard strips. Ask a grown-up to poke a paper fastener through the center of each X.

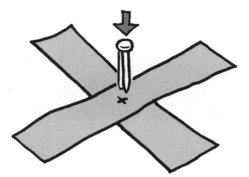

2 Connect the ends of the strips as shown in the finished pincers.

3 Cut two halves of a claw from orange paper. Decorate with marker. Glue onto the cardboard ends. Open and shut the pincers!

CRABBY CRABS!

CRABBY COUNTING

Crabs are members of a large group of animals without a backbone, like insects and spiders. They all have hard outside skeletons, jointed legs, and a body that is divided into parts!

TRY IT: Count how many legs a spider has. Now count how many legs a crab has (don't count the pincers). Do they have the same number of legs? What else do they have in common?

DO THE CRAB WALK!

Put your hands and feet under you, with your chest facing up. Now, walk sideways like a crab. How fast can you go?

Manatee

What you need

Scissors (for grown-up use)
Large athletic sock, white or gray or any color
String
Fiberfil or cotton stuffing
Fabric or tacky glue
Black marker

WHAT YOU DO

1 Have a grown-up cut the cuff off the sock. Tie string around the toe of the sock for the manatee's tail.

2 Stuff the sock. Glue the end of the sock closed.

3 Cut out two flippers from the cuff of the sock. Glue them onto the sides of the manatee. Use marker to draw the manatee's eyes, nostrils, and mouth.

SLOW — MANATEES AHEAD!

Manatees graze
in the sea grass in warm,
shallow water near sandy shores,
such as in protected bays
and sea canals.
Unfortunately,
those are the same places
where boats travel fast,
and the gentle,
slow-moving manatees
often get injured if they
don't move out of the way.
In Florida,
there are laws to protect
the endangered manatee.
Signs in the water
tell people to drive their
motorboats slowly,
so they won't hit
a manatee!

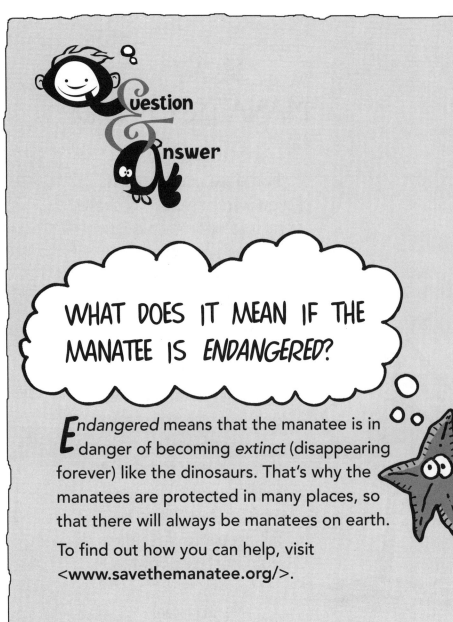

Question & Answer

WHAT DOES IT MEAN IF THE MANATEE IS *ENDANGERED?*

*E*ndangered means that the manatee is in danger of becoming *extinct* (disappearing forever) like the dinosaurs. That's why the manatees are protected in many places, so that there will always be manatees on earth.

To find out how you can help, visit <www.savethemanatee.org/>.

WHO AM I?

Manatees aren't fish, they're *mammals*. Like all other mammals, they breathe air through their nostrils into their lungs, give birth to live babies, and nurse their young with milk. Look in a mirror. Do you see another mammal? That's right, you!

IN THE TIDE POOL

Sea creatures that live in tide pools
are really very brave.
At first they lie out in the sun,
Then they're covered by a wave!

Tide Scene

THE TIDE RUSHES IN
WITH A WAVE AND A ROAR.
THEN IT SLOWLY DRIFTS OUT
AWAY FROM THE SHORE.

What you need

Large white paper plate
Pencil
Blue construction paper
Child safety scissors
Glue
Markers
Paper fastener

LiTTLe HANDS STORY CORNER™

Out of the Ocean
BY DEBRA FRASIER

In One Tidepool
BY ANTHONY D. FREDERICKS

WHAT YOU DO

1 Turn the paper plate upside down. Trace around it onto the blue paper. Cut out the circle. Cut the circle in half with a wavy line.

2 Glue one blue half onto the paper plate. Draw sea creatures on the white side.

3 Use the paper fastener to attach the other blue half circle through the center of the plate as shown on page 52. Draw waves with a marker.

4 Turn the blue paper to cover the sea creatures at high tide. Uncover them at low tide!

Question & Answer

WHY DOES THE TIDE COME IN AND THEN GO OUT?

The *tide* — the rise and fall of the ocean — is caused by the pull of the moon and sun on the water. At high tide, the shore is covered by salt water. At low tide, the shore is uncovered and you can see all the seaweed and shells that washed in with the tide. *Tide pools* are miniature ponds of the salt water that get trapped on the rocky beach, along with all the fascinating sea creatures that live there!

CHANGING TIDES

A PRETEND TIDE POOL

Sometimes at an aquarium you can touch the creatures that live there. Imagine brushing against a prickly sea urchin (page 55)!

To make a pretend tide pool, ask an adult to fill a pan with about an inch of water. Add a plastic scrub brush (as a sea urchin), a kitchen sponge (as a live sponge animal), seashells or pennies, and small plastic sea creatures. Close your eyes and put your hands under the water. Name the sea creatures that might live in a tide pool just by touching these pretend ones!

TIDE POOL PLAY

In a tide pool, things can change quickly! When the tide is in, the water is cooler and filled with fresh food. When the tide is out, the pool gets warm and salty. The tide pool might even begin to dry up causing the critters to move under rocks and seaweed to keep their bodies moist.

Take a tide pool bath! When you're taking a bath, pretend you're in a warm, salty tide pool.

Slowly let the "tide" go down the drain as you just sit there. What does it feel like? That happens several times every day to tide pool creatures, and they have no towels!

QUICK CHANGE!

People have to adjust to outside changes, too — when it suddenly begins to rain, or when the temperature in the morning is cold but by afternoon it is warm. Luckily, people don't have to make a lot of fast changes. Tide pool critters adjust to big changes several times a day!

TRY IT: Pretend it's winter and draw a picture of what you would wear. Now it's summer — draw a picture of you on a sunny day!

Sea Urchin

> IN CRACKS IN ROCKS
> BELOW THE TIDE,
> SNACKING ON SEAWEED,
> SEA URCHINS HIDE!

What you need

Play Clay (see below)
Red and blue food coloring
Waxed paper
Bright-colored toothpicks

Play Clay
2 cups (500 ml) flour
1 cup (250 ml) salt
3/4 to 1 cup (175 to 250 ml) water
2 tablespoons (25 ml) vegetable oil

In a bowl, mix together the flour and salt. Slowly add the water and the oil to the flour mix. Stir until a dough forms.

WHAT YOU DO

1 Prepare the clay dough, adding a few drops of red and blue food coloring to the water as you make it. Working on the waxed paper, roll the dough into a ball.

2 Poke toothpicks into the ball.

3 Allow the clay to air-dry or have a grown-up bake it at 300°F (150°C) until hardened.

. . . .

small fry **FUN**

For an edible urchin, poke pretzel sticks in a marshmallow and then eat it!

URCHIN FUN!

WALK LIKE AN URCHIN

Urchins use their spines like hundreds of tiny legs. They look as if they're walking on stilts!

TRY IT: Ask a grown-up to make a hole in both sides of two empty coffee cans. Thread rope through the holes. Hold onto the rope and try walking on the can stilts!

CREATE AN URCHIN CAVE

The sea urchin also uses its prickly spines to carve a home in the tide pool's rocks.

TRY IT: Make yourself a cave out of chairs and a blanket. Now, pretend you're a sea urchin, safe inside. How small of a ball can you curl up into?

Hermit Crab Home

What you need

2 small paper bowls
Child safety scissors
Markers
Glue

A House for Hermit Crab
BY ERIC CARLE

The Sea House
BY DEBORAH TURNEY ZAGWYN

WHAT YOU DO

1 In the bottom of one paper bowl, cut a hole large enough to fit your hand through. Cut out an opening in the side of the bowl. (Ask a grown-up to help you cut.)

2 Decorate the outside of the second bowl with markers. Glue it upside down on top of the first bowl.

3 Put your hand through the hole in the bottom of the bowl. Poke your fingers out the side opening. Wiggle your fingers to make the crab "walk." If you like, use different colors and patterns to decorate a larger set of bowls for a new hermit crab home!

Animal Helpers

In nature, many creatures work together to help one another. The sea anemone (page 68) sometimes hitches a ride on a hermit crab's home! The anemone's stinging tentacles help protect the hermit crab from being eaten by fish, and the sea anemone gets a free ride!

Think of ways you help others and ways that others help you. Who makes your dinner? If you pick up your toys or help sort the laundry, you're a helper too. Good for you!

Question & Answer

I THOUGHT A "HERMIT" DIDN'T LIKE TO BE AROUND OTHERS. IS A HERMIT CRAB UNFRIENDLY?

Hermit crabs aren't really "hermits" at all. They are very friendly! So friendly, in fact, that they make themselves right at home in the empty shells of other creatures. Visit a pet store or an aquarium to see hermit crabs carrying their "borrowed" homes on their backs.

What other creatures carry their homes on their backs? A snail does. Now *you* think of one. (Hint: Think of an animal that was in a famous race with a rabbit and won!)

Important! Hermit crabs might appear as if they could live anywhere. But ocean hermit crabs need to be in the ocean, so never take them from a beach. They will die before you even get home!

ACT LIKE A HERMIT CRAB!

The seashell that I live in
(hands together above head)
I've suddenly outgrown.
(hands held down at side)
I'll find a shell that no one wants
(shake head side to side)
And make it all my own!
(cross arms over chest)

Sea Star

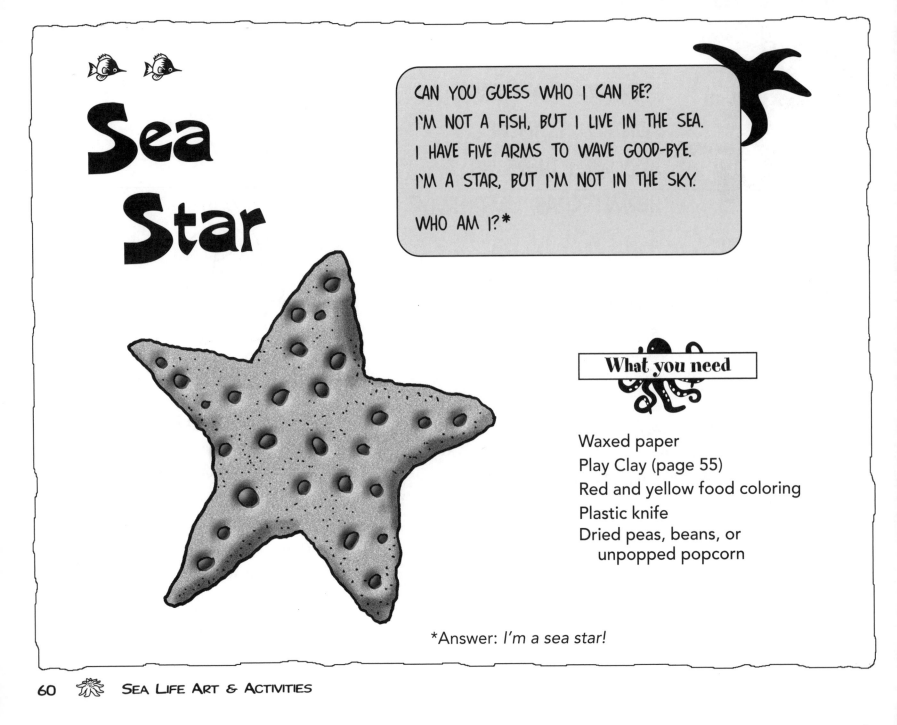

CAN YOU GUESS WHO I CAN BE?
I'M NOT A FISH, BUT I LIVE IN THE SEA.
I HAVE FIVE ARMS TO WAVE GOOD-BYE.
I'M A STAR, BUT I'M NOT IN THE SKY.

WHO AM I?*

What you need

Waxed paper
Play Clay (page 55)
Red and yellow food coloring
Plastic knife
Dried peas, beans, or
  unpopped popcorn

*Answer: *I'm a sea star!*

WHAT YOU DO

1 Cover your work surface with waxed paper. Prepare the clay dough, adding a few drops of the food coloring to tint the dough. Shape the clay into a pancake. Use the plastic knife to cut out the sea star's arms.

2 Press the dried beans, seeds, or popcorn into the arms for spiny skin.

3 Let the clay air-dry to harden or ask a grown-up to bake it in a 300°F (150°C) oven.

• •

small fry **FUN**

Cut a sea star from a kitchen sponge. Dip the sponge into orange, brown, red, or purple tempera paint. Press onto paper for a sea star print.

LITTLE HANDS STORY CORNER™

A Star at the Bottom of the Sea
BY GAYLE RIDINGER

Starfish
BY EDITH THACHER HURD

Sea Star Shapes

Sea stars aren't fish. They are spiny animals with arms that point out like a star (that's why we call them sea *stars* instead of star*fish*). Most sea stars have five *rays* (arms), but some have 10 or more. No matter how many rays it has, though, a sea star is always shaped like a wheel with the rays pointing out from the center.

Make sea star spaghetti art!
Draw a dot in the center of a large sheet of paper. Place dry spaghetti in the shape of a wheel radiating out from the dot. Count the "spokes" of the wheel. How many rays does your sea star have? Paint the spaghetti rays, let them dry, and glue them to the paper for a raised sea star picture.

Have Fun with Tongue Twisters!

Try to say each of these silly sea sayings one time slowly. Then try saying them five times, really fast! Make up some of your own!

- *Sunbeams shine through tide pools and spotlight spiny starfish.*

- *She sells seashells by the sea shore.*

- *Pretty purple sea urchins live in a tide pool with periwinkles.*

- *The tricky tide tried to tickle Terri's ten toes.*

Question & Answer

I SAW A SEA STAR THAT HAD A REALLY TINY RAY, DIFFERENT FROM ALL OF ITS OTHER ONES. WAS IT SICK?

When a sea star loses one of its rays (from a bite by another sea creature, for instance), it simply grows a new one! The little ray you saw was the growing ray. If people lose limbs, we can't regrow them, of course. But what happens when you skin your knee? Does new skin grow over the scrape?

Suction Power!

Sea stars use suction tubes on the undersides of their rays to pry open clam and mussel shells and to slowly move around. You can try out suction power, too!

Press a straw against a square of paper and suck in hard, until the paper comes off the table. That's suction power!

A coral reef's like a garden,
Growing under the sea.
Colorful fish dart in and out
Between the *"a-neh-ma-nee"!

THE CORAL REEF

* anemone (page 68)

Colorful Coral

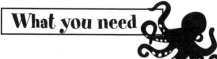

What you need

Child safety scissors
Construction paper
Markers
Clear plastic drinking cup
Glue
Kitchen sponge
Red, green, yellow, and blue tempera
   paint, in separate dishes or lids

WHAT YOU DO

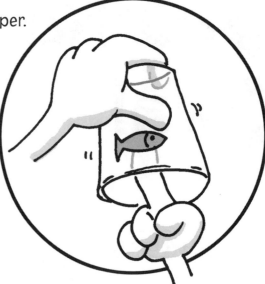

1 Cut out small fish and other sea life from the paper. Decorate with markers.

2 Hold the plastic cup upside down in one hand. Glue the fish facing outward inside the cup.

3 Dip the sponge in paint. Dab around the outside of the cup for coral.

4 Set your coral reef on a shelf for all to see!

• •

small fry FUN

Cut out fish. Glue to blue construction paper. Dip a sponge into tempera paint and dab around the fish for coral.

Walk on the Great Barrier Reef
BY CAROLINE ARNOLD

Hello, Fish: Visiting the Coral Reef
BY SYLVIA A. EARLE

IS CORAL A TREE OR A FISH?

Neither! Coral sometimes looks like branching trees, waving in the water. But guess what? Coral isn't a plant at all. Coral is made from the skeletons of many tiny animals called *polyps* (PA-lips). Each polyp builds a chalky, cup-shaped shelter (an outer skeleton) to protect its soft body. As young polyps build new shelters on the skeletons of dead polyps, the reef gets bigger!

Build a tower of building blocks with a friend. How tall is your tower? How many blocks did you use? Now, add more towers to your tower to make a pretend reef.

REEFS IN DANGER

How long did it take you to make your towers? It takes thousands of years for a coral reef to form. Sometimes the reefs grow less than an inch (cm) a year! Unfortunately, many coral reefs are destroyed by pollution or people breaking off the coral.

TO LEARN MORE ABOUT CORAL REEFS,

go to this exhibit at the Monterey Bay Aquarium's website: <**www.mbayaq.org/efc/ efc_se/sz_rrh_coral.asp**>.

Sea Anemone

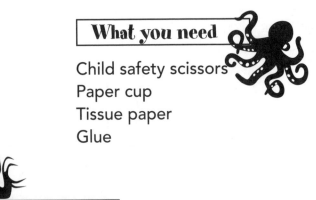

WHAT YOU DO

1 Cut the paper cup as shown. Cut a long strip of tissue paper twice as tall as the cup bottom.

2 Wrap the tissue paper around the cup bottom. Glue to hold.

3 Cut fringe along the top edge of the tissue paper as shown on the finished anemone.

LITTLE ANEMONE*

I look just like a flower,
(hands together)
Sitting in the sea.
(spread fingers apart)
I wave hello as fish swim by,
(wave hands)
I hope they'll visit me!
I welcome them with open arms,
(wiggle fingers)
Then take a great big bite.
(close hands quickly)
Fish taste so delicious,
(rub tummy)
I eat them every night!

* ah-NEH-ma-nee

PLAY SEA-LIFE GAMES!

BE A SEA ANEMONE

Two players face each other with their arms raised and hands joined to form an arch. They're the anemone. A third player, the fish, walks around the anemone and under the arch. All the players say the poem on this page. At the words, "I eat them every night," the anemone players lower their arms and try to "catch" the fish. Trade places, so each player gets to be the fish.

Angelfish

ANGELFISH DO NOT HAVE WINGS,
AND THEY CAN'T EVEN FLY.
BUT DIVE DOWN TO A CORAL REEF
AND YOU'LL SEE THEM SWIMMING BY!

What you need

Child safety scissors

Plastic egg carton

Construction paper (all colors, including blue)

Markers

Glue

Toothpicks

Scraps of green tissue paper

WHAT YOU DO

1 Cut a three-cup section from the egg carton. Cut out angelfish from construction paper. Decorate the fish with markers.

2 Glue each fish onto one end of a toothpick. Poke the toothpick into the egg carton.

3 Cut out waves from blue construction paper. Glue onto the front of the egg carton.

4 Glue the tissue paper onto the tooth-picks for seaweed. Poke into the egg carton.

Play Go Fish!

Each player gets five cards, facedown. The remaining cards go in a "fish pile." To begin, each player lays down any matching pairs in his hand. Then Player #1 asks Player #2 for a card that matches one of her cards ("Derek, do you have any threes?"). If Player #2 has any cards that match (a three, in this case), he hands it over. Player #1 puts the pair of matching cards down and asks Player #3 for a match to another card she has. If Player #3 doesn't have it, he says, "Go fish!" Player #1 then takes the top card from the fish pile. If it's a match, Player #1 puts that pair down, too, and keeps asking. If it's not a match, Player #3 starts asking other players for cards. Continue until a player has set down all his cards or the fish pile is used up. The player with the most card pairs is the winner.

Giant Clam

IF YOU WANT TO SEE A CLAM,
TELL IT TO OPEN WIDE.
IT'S HIDING IN BETWEEN ITS SHELLS,
TUCKED HAPPILY INSIDE!

What you need

White paper
Child safety scissors
Blue and brown tempera paint
Paintbrushes
Black marker

A Clam Named Sam
BY LEE DEVITT

WHAT YOU DO

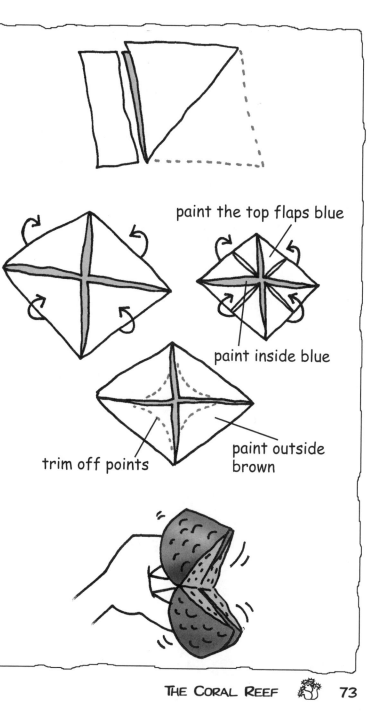

paint the top flaps blue

paint inside blue

trim off points

paint outside brown

1 Fold the white paper in half to make a triangle. Trim off the extra. Now you have a square. Unfold the paper and lay it flat.

2 Fold each corner into the center; leave it folded. Turn the square over and fold each new corner to the center. This will be the inside of the clam. Paint the inside and top of the flaps blue; let dry.

3 Turn the paper back over. Cut off the points of the flaps.

4 Paint the outside of the clam brown. Use black marker to draw ridges on the shell.

5 Put your fingers in the brown flaps. Open and close the shell.

CLAM FUN

SHELL CHECK!

What do clams and scallops have in common? They both have a hinged shell that can open and close, protecting the soft animal that lives inside. **TRY IT:** With a grown-up's permission, put a hard-boiled egg in a zip-locking bag. Drop the egg on the floor. Did the shell crack? Now, put another hard-boiled egg in a plastic container with a lid and drop it on the floor. Which worked better to protect the egg, the soft bag or the hard plastic container? If you were a soft clam, which outer covering would you rather have — hard or soft?

PLAY I SPY

What things can you see around your house or school that have hinges so they open and close like a clam shell? Think about what you carry clothes in on a long trip away from home. Can you find any other containers that open and close like a clam?

Question & **A**nswer

HOW "GIANT" IS A GIANT CLAM?

Some giant clams are 4 feet (1.2 m) long and weigh more than 500 pounds (227 kg). That's about as tall as you and as heavy as a pony!

Hello!

DON'T BE FOOLED BY THIS LETTUCE,
IT'S NOT A TASTY TREAT.
IT'S REALLY A SEA CREATURE
THAT YOU DON'T WANT TO EAT!

Lettuce Sea Slug

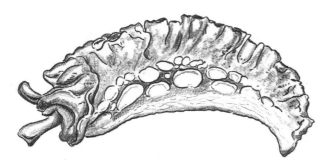

What you need

Green marker
White construction paper
Green tissue paper
Pencil
Glue

WHAT YOU DO

1 Draw a slug shape on the white paper.

2 Tear the green tissue paper into small pieces. Curl the pieces around the head of the pencil.

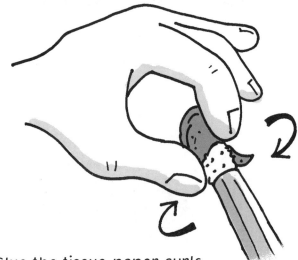

3 Glue the tissue-paper curls to the slug shape.

4 Draw seaweed and coral around the slug.

MAKE SOME SLIME!

Lettuce sea slugs look like
a tasty salad,
but their skins produce a slime
that tastes yucky!

TO MAKE YOUR OWN SLIME,
combine
3/4 cup (175 ml) cornstarch
and
1/2 cup (125 ml) water.
The slime will thicken the more
you play with it.
Add more water to make it slimier.
Now, close your eyes
and describe what slime feels like.
Is it silky smooth
or gritty?
Is it thick or thin?

Kelp waves in the water,
anchored against the tide.
In its cool and leafy shelter
Fish and otters like to hide!

THE KELP FOREST

Giant Kelp

KELP'S A KIND OF SEAWEED
(NOT A PLANT YOU HAVE TO SOW).
IT BECOMES A FOREST
WHEN IT STARTS TO GROW!

What you need

Child safety scissors
White and green construction paper
Markers
Tape

WHAT YOU DO

1 Cut the white construction paper into strips 2" (5 cm) wide. Draw fish swimming across each paper strip. Draw kelp growing on the green paper.

cut here ------

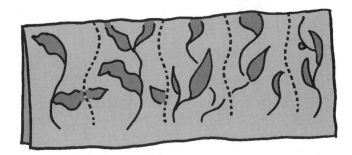

2 Fold the green construction paper in half as shown. Cut wavy slits across the paper, stopping about 1" (2.5 cm) from the edge.

3 Weave the white paper strips in and out of the green slits. Tape the ends to hold.

The Hidden Forest
BY JEANNIE BAKER

Question & Answer

WHAT IS KELP, AND WHY IS IT A GIANT?

Giant kelp belongs to a group of plants called *algae* (AL-gee). Algae can be tiny green specks in the water, or they can grow big (like a giant!) and form an ocean forest. Giant kelp is one of the fastest-growing plants in the world, growing as much as 2 feet (60 cm) in one day!

How big are you growing?
Ask a grown-up to measure how tall you are and how much you weigh. Compare it to how big you were a year ago, or when you were born. How much have you grown?

Create Habitat Puzzles

Giant kelp forests are an important habitat (the place where an animal or plant lives, page 20). Lots of sea animals live in this hidden ocean forest!

Color a picture of sea creatures you might find hiding in a kelp forest on one sheet of paper. On a second paper, glue cutout pictures of trees and animals you might find hiding in a forest on land. Have a grown-up glue each picture to a piece of cardboard and cut it into puzzle pieces. Match the pieces together, putting the animals into the right habitat!

SIZE FUN!

BIG PLANT, LITTLE PLANT

Go on a nature walk with a grown-up. Look above you for plants that are *big*. Can you name any of the tallest plants you see? Crouch down on the ground. What *little* plants do you see?

TRY IT: Plant a bean seed or sunflower seed in a pot filled with soil. Put it in a sunny window and water it. Watch it grow! Measure how tall it gets.

SIZE SORT

Organize a group of items, such as your stuffed animals or books, according to size from *big to little*. Start with the largest book or animal and put it next to one that's smaller. Keep sorting until you've sorted all the items. Now, mix them up and sort from *littlest to biggest*.

Sea Otter Mask

What you need

Child safety scissors
Large white paper plate
Yarn or ribbon
Black and brown markers
White paper
Glue

Pup's Supper
BY VICTORIA MILES

WHAT YOU DO

1 Cut out a sea otter mask as shown on page 82 from the paper plate. Cut openings for the eyes.

2 Poke a hole on both sides of the mask. Tie yarn or ribbon through the holes.

3 Draw the sea otter's fur, nose, and ears.

4 Cut thin strips of white paper for whiskers. Glue to plate.

THE SEA OTTER'S SONG

Floating, floating in the sea,
Otters swimming merrily.
(pretend to swim with arms)
Listen to the crack, crack, crack
Of otters eating on their backs.
(pretend to eat)
Grooming, grooming their fur coats,
(comb hair)
Otters see some fishing boats.
(peer out with hand on forehead)
Let's all sing the sea otter's song,
Use your hands to clap along!

Question & Answer

SEA OTTERS LOOK LIKE FURRY PUPPIES OR KITTENS. WHAT KIND OF ANIMAL ARE THEY?

Otters do have a lot of fur — a double layer, in fact! That fur keeps their bodies warm in the cold ocean, but they have to keep it very clean, just like a cat does. An otter spends about five hours a day grooming its fur!

Otter babies are called *pups*. They must come up to the surface to breathe air (an otter is really good at holding its breath underwater). An otter is a *mammal*, just like you and your dog or cat!

OTTER FUN!

Otters are very curious and like to have fun in the water. Floating on its back, a sea otter uses its tummy as a table. With its paws, it uses a rock to hammer its shellfish dinner open. Sea otters sleep on their backs, too, resting on the water in big groups called *rafts*.

PLAY "HA, HA"

Have some "raft fun" with your friends!

TRY IT: Everybody lies down on his or her back on the floor, one person's head on another person's tummy. One person starts by saying, "Ha, Ha!" The next person repeats the phrase, then adds his own "Ha, Ha!" As the "Ha, Ha!" continues, pretty soon everyone will be giggling!

Brown Turban Snail

I CRAWL ALONG THE TOWERING KELP,
I'M QUIET AS A MOUSE.
I NIBBLE, NIBBLE AS I GO,
CARRYING MY HAT-SHAPED HOUSE!

WHO AM I?*

What you need

Play Clay (page 55)
Kitchen sponge
Brown tempera paint,
   in dish or lid

*Answer: *An ocean snail!*

The Biggest House in the World
BY LEO LIONNI

WHAT YOU DO

1 Roll clay into a long snake. Coil the clay so it looks like a turban.

2 Allow clay to air-dry, or have a grown-up bake it at 300°F (150°C) until hardened.

3 Dip the sponge in the paint. Press onto the snail.

CRAWL LIKE A SNAIL!

Sit on the ground with your feet and legs in front of you close together. Curl your body up over your legs in a ball, like the snail's shell. Inch forward, using your feet and legs as one big foot. How fast can you go?

IS A SEA SNAIL LIKE THE GARDEN SNAIL I SEE IN MY YARD?

A garden snail and a sea snail are a lot alike (they're cousins!).

Put a garden snail or a slug (another close relative) into a glass jar. Look closely at the bottom of it as it climbs the side of the jar. Can you see a slimy trail? In what ways are a garden snail and a sea snail different? Well, your garden snail crawls on land plants, while a sea snail slides along on kelp in the water!

I'M AN OCEAN GOLDFISH

I'm a goldfish in the sea,
(swim like a fish)

Just as pretty as can be.
(cup face in hands)

My tail is really quite a sight,
(swish hand like a tail)

My orange color's very bright.
(circle fingers around eyes)

I swim alone in the deep,
(swim like a fish)

And when I'm tired I go to sleep!
(rest head on arm)

What you need

Orange and blue construction paper
Pencil
Child safety scissors
Glue
Markers

Garibaldi Fish

WHAT YOU DO

1 Fold the orange paper in half the long way. Draw half hearts along the folded edge. Draw ovals along the open edge.

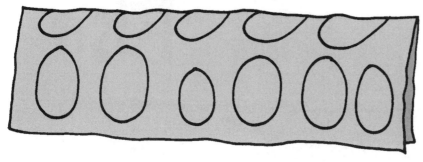

2 Cut out the shapes. Glue them onto the blue paper to make fish.

3 Use markers to draw the fishes' eyes, mouths, gills, and fins.

small fry **FUN**

Cut out an oval and heart from orange paper. Glue to blue paper. Add blue spots on the fish with a marker.

Fish Eyes: A Book You Can Count On BY LOIS EHLERT

The Rainbow Fish BY MARCUS PFISTER

Question & Answer

WE HAVE GOLDFISH IN A FISH TANK AT SCHOOL. ARE THEY GARIBALDI FISH?

GARIBALDI   GOLDFISH

Probably not. The small yellow or gold fish known as the common goldfish is a different fish than the garibaldi fish, or ocean goldfish. There are all different kinds of goldfish, and they live in different places. Some like warm water, others like cooler water; some like salty water, and some like fresh (unsalty) water. The garibaldi fish is very big — a foot (30 cm) long! It lives in kelp forests and on reefs off the coast of California. You can't miss its bright orange color!

COLOR FUN!

FISH FAMILY ART

If you were a garibaldi fish, you'd sure spend a lot of time with your dad! In this fish family, the daddy fish guards the fish eggs and the young. The baby garibaldi fish have bright blue spots. That way, the dads know the babies are not an intruding adult fish that should be attacked.

TRY IT: Paint a picture of an orange daddy garibaldi fish next to some smaller orange fish. Cut out blue spots from construction paper and glue to the smaller fish.

LET'S GO KIDS.

THE OPEN SEA

Much of our planet is open sea
Where graceful "jellies" drift by.
Dolphins and turtles swim back and forth,
And the sailfish seem to fly!

Jellyfish (Sea Jelly)

WATCH AS THE JELLYFISH SLOWLY GOES BY —
IT'S QUITE AN AMAZING THING.
IT'S SHAPED LIKE A BELL THAT IS CRYSTAL CLEAR,
WITH LONG TENTACLES THAT STING!

What you need

Child safety scissors
Blue construction paper
Tape
Waxed paper
Markers

Jellyfish
BY MARTHA E. H. RUSTAD

WHAT YOU DO

1 Have a grown-up help you cut circle shapes in the blue paper (don't cut through the edge of the paper).

2 Tape waxed paper across the back of the paper, covering the holes, to make the sea jelly "bells."

3 Tear pieces of waxed paper into strips. Tape to the bottoms of the bells for the tentacles.

4 Draw fish on the paper with markers.

. . . .

small fry FUN Cut out a jellyfish from waxed paper. Tape on ribbon tentacles.

Question & Answer

IS A JELLYFISH MADE OF JELLY? AND WHY DOES IT HAVE TWO NAMES?

You don't want to eat this jelly! A jellyfish isn't made of the yummy jelly you eat — its body just looks like a big blob of clear jelly. And you don't want to get near a jellyfish at the beach. If you touch its tentacles, you may get stung. Ouch!

The correct name of the jellyfish is now "sea jelly." That's because the sea jelly isn't a fish — it doesn't have a backbone like a fish (page 11).

SEA JELLY FUN

FLOAT OR SINK?

The sea jelly is so light that it floats on water, moving with the wind, waves, and currents.

TRY IT: Blow air into a zip-locking plastic sandwich bag and seal it shut to make a sea jelly. Ask a grown-up to fill a small basin or tub with water. Float your sea jelly in the water and blow hard on the plastic bag. Can you make your sea jelly move across the water?

SQUISHY STUFF

With no bones, a sea jelly's body is very squishy.

TRY IT: Put a few spoonfuls of jelly into a cup. Now, close your eyes and feel the jelly with your fingers. Is it firm or squishy? Can you guess how the sea jelly got its name?

MAKE A MUSCLE!

The sea jelly has strong muscles in its bell-shaped body that push out water, moving the sea jelly along to where it needs to go. You wouldn't want to feel a sea jelly's muscle, but you can feel one of your own.

TRY IT: Bend one arm up at the elbow. Can you feel the muscle in your upper arm with your other hand?

Sea Turtle Puppet

What you need

Child safety scissors

Green or brown construction paper

Marker

Tape

Glue

Old black sock

2 safety pins

Into the Sea BY BRENDA Z. GUIBERSON

Little Turtle and the Song of the Sea
BY SHERIDAN CAIN

Sea Turtles BY GAIL GIBBONS

WHAT YOU DO

1 Cut out a circle from the paper for the turtle's shell. Cut a slit in both ends. Overlap the cut ends slightly and tape to hold.

2 Cut out the turtle's tail, feet, eyes, and nose. Tape the tail and feet onto the shell. Draw a pattern on the turtle's shell. Draw scaly skin on the feet.

3 Glue the turtle's eyes and nose to the top of the sock toe. Ask a grown-up to pin the turtle's shell onto the sock. Put your hand inside for a puppet.

• •

Use puffy fabric paint to draw a turtle on an old white sock. Let dry. Put your hand inside the sock for a puppet.

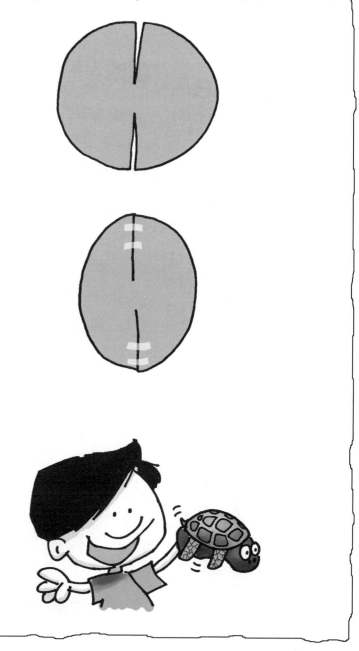

BE A SEA TURTLE!

The sea turtle swims in the ocean,
(swimming motion)
Then slowly comes ashore.
(walk with fingers)
The thing that's so amazing is —
(hands apart, palms up)
It knows where it's been before!
(clap hands)

IS A SEA TURTLE A FISH OR A TURTLE?

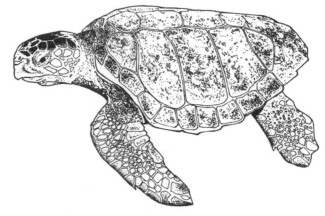

The sea turtle swims, but it isn't a fish. It's a *reptile*, just like land turtles and alligators!

SEA TURTLE FUN

BABY TURTLES AHEAD!

At nesting time, green sea turtles travel hundreds of miles (km) to the beach where they were born to lay their eggs. After they hatch, the baby turtles crawl out of their nests at night (when it's less likely they will be eaten) and head straight for the sea, guided by the moon's light on the water.

TRY IT: Take a walk with a grown-up outdoors when the moon is bright, or indoors in a darkened room with only a flashlight shining. Together, find your way carefully in the dim light, using all your senses. How do things *look* different? What can you *feel* around you? Stand still. Do you *smell* grass or flowers or dinner cooking? What do you *hear*? Birds or crickets, a car or an airplane, or people talking? Imagine being a baby turtle, finding your way to the sea for the first time at night!

TURTLE COUNT

Beach development (like buildings and roads) destroys the places sea turtles raise their young (their *habitats*, page 20), and hunting of the sea turtles has left fewer and fewer sea turtles alive in the ocean. Certain sea turtles are *endangered*, or in danger of becoming extinct.

TRY IT: Ask a grown-up to hide 50 dried beans around a room. Look for the hidden beans. How many did you find? Now search again. How many beans did you find this time? Search a third time. Now how many beans did you find? Each time it gets harder and harder to find the beans because there are fewer and fewer of them.

Sailfish

SAILFISH SKIM ACROSS THE OCEAN,
A FIN'S ALL YOU MAY SEE.
THESE SPEEDY FISH ARE AMAZING —
MUCH FASTER THAN YOU OR ME!

What you need

Blue construction paper
Tape
Child safety scissors
Black marker

WHAT YOU DO

leave this part unrolled

1 Roll the blue construction paper partway into a tube, leaving the upper half unrolled as shown. Tape to hold. Cut across one end of the tube as shown. Tape the edges together.

roll into tube

2 Cut the sail-like fin from the unrolled paper.

3 Cut out the sailfish's pointed jaw and tail fin from the paper scraps. Tape onto the sailfish. Use marker to draw the sailfish's eye, fin, and fin spots.

cut end

• •

small fry
FUN

Cut out a rectangle from blue construction paper for a sailfish body. Tape it to white paper. Add a blue triangle for its fin. Use blue marker to draw the sailfish's tail fin and pointed jaw.

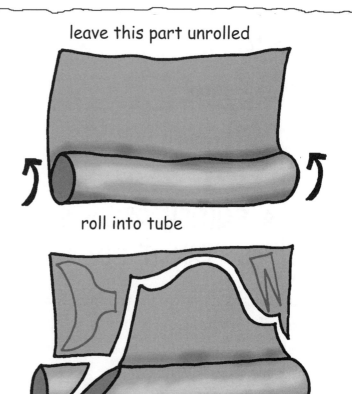

Question & Answer

DOES A SAILFISH REALLY SAIL?
HOW FAST CAN IT GO?

A sailfish uses its large fin to catch the breeze like the sail on a boat. At 68 miles per hour (109 kph), a sailfish zips along as fast as a car on a freeway! It's the fastest fish in the sea.

When you're riding in a car, ask the driver to tell you how fast you are going. Now imagine a sailfish swimming alongside the car, going even faster than you are!

Cool!

SHAPE FUN!

SHAPE ART

Have a grown-up help you cut out squares, ovals, triangles, circles, and rectangles from construction paper. Use some of the shapes to make a sailboat shape. Glue the sailboat onto paper. What shapes would you use to make a car or a building? Make more shape-art pictures.

MAKE (AND SAIL!) A MINI-SAILBOAT

Tape a large paper triangle to a plastic straw. Poke a toothpick into a plastic-foam tray (from fruits and vegetables only). Slide the straw over the toothpick to hold the sail in place. Ask a grown-up to put a small amount of water in a basin or brownie pan. Then, sail your boat. What happens when you blow on the sail? Have a sailboat race with a friend to see whose boat goes faster!

DOLPHINS NEVER SEEM TO TIRE,
THEY REALLY LOVE TO PLAY!
THROUGH THE WAVES THEY LEAP AND DIVE,
AS THEY FROLIC THROUGH THE DAY.

Dolphin

What you need

Watercolor paint
Paintbrush
Large white paper plate
Tape
Child safety scissors
Blue construction paper
Drinking straw

WHAT YOU DO

 1 Paint the paper plate to look like the sea. Let dry.

2 Fold the plate in half. Tape the lower corners together. Have a grown-up cut a slit in the center fold.

3 Cut a dolphin from the paper. Tape to the end of the straw.

4 Slide the straw through the slit in the fold. Move the end back and forth so your dolphin leaps over the waves.

tape here

cut slit here

tape here

Question & Answer

I'VE HEARD THAT DOLPHINS ARE REALLY SMART ANIMALS. CAN THEY TALK?

Dolphins don't have vocal cords the way we do, but they make whistles, clicking sounds, moans, squeals, and squeaks from their throats. Some sounds they make our ears can't even hear. Many people believe that dolphins have their own language.

What sounds can you make? Click your tongue to make a dolphin-like sound, or practice whistling.

DOLPHIN GAMES!

DOLPHIN CATCH

Do you like to play? So do dolphins! One of their favorite games is catch. They throw a seaweed "toy" in the air, then carry it in their mouths, or pass it back and forth. Or they may play tug-of-war with it with a sea lion!

TRY IT: Bounce or throw a big ball or a bean bag back and forth with a friend. Leap in the air like a dolphin as you play!

DO AS DOLPHINS DO!

Mother dolphins keep an eye on their babies every minute of the day and night. They swim together, matching their movements. If the mother dives, the baby dives, if the mother turns, the baby turns, and if the mother comes to the surface for a breath, the baby does too!

TRY IT: Play "Dolphin Says" with your friends. One player is chosen to be the leader. The other "dolphins" imitate the actions of the leader only when he says out loud, "Dolphins, do this." If the leader says, "Do this" without saying "Dolphins" first, any dolphin that tries to copy him is out of the game.

If you go down deep into the sea,
You'll find it's as dark as night.
Strange fish that glow and giant squid
are quite an awesome sight!

IN THE DEEP

WAY DOWN IN THE DEEP, DARK SEA,
DAY TURNS INTO NIGHT.
IF THIS FISH HAS LOST ITS WAY,
IT SWITCHES ON A LIGHT!

Lantern Fish

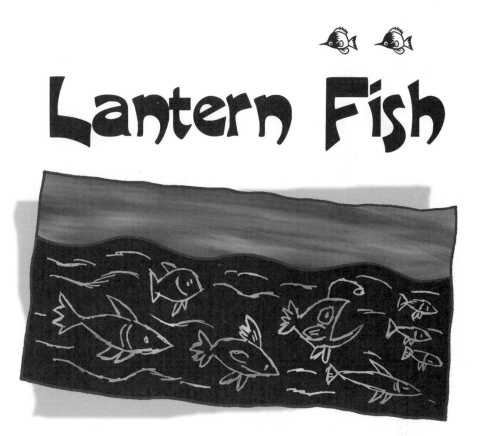

What you need

Child safety scissors
White envelope
Crayons, including blue and black
Toothpick or paper clip

WHAT YOU DO

1   Cut off the envelope's flap. Cut a wavy line along the edge of the envelope's pocket.

2   Color the top half of the envelope blue. Cover the lower half of the envelope with bright colors, pressing down hard for rich, thick color. Color over the bright colors with black crayon.

3   Scratch fish into the black crayon surface.

DOES A LANTERN FISH REALLY CARRY A LANTERN?

Not the way you and I carry lanterns! These small fish have special parts on their sides and bellies that brighten their way, like miniature built-in flashlights! The lights also make the outline of the fish harder to see, confusing the fish's enemies.

LIGHT GAMES!

At dusk, when night is falling, it's harder to see. Shapes blur into the background. This is how it looks deep underwater, too, where there's just a faint bluish light.

FLASHLIGHT TAG

Play flashlight tag outdoors at dusk. Each player has a grown-up partner so that you can find your way safely in the dim light. The pair of players who are "It" is given a flashlight while the other players run to hide. A player is caught when "It" shines the flashlight on him.

PUT ON A LIGHT SHOW!

Cut out a fish shape in the bottom of a paper cup. Place the cup over a flashlight. Turn off the lights and aim the flashlight on a nearby wall. Move the flashlight back and forth to see your fish swim in the deep, dark sea. Include friends with more fish cutouts!

Octopus

What you need

Child safety scissors

Brown paper lunch bag

Paper cup

Tape

Marker

Pencil

Wiggly eyes and glue (optional)

Crayons (optional)

Little Hands Story Corner™

How to Hide an Octopus & Other Sea Creatures by Ruth Heller

An Octopus Is Amazing by Patricia Lauber

WHAT YOU DO

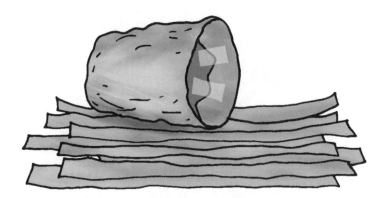

1 Cut open the bag and lay it flat. Wrap the cup in the bag. Cut off the extra, leaving just enough to fold over the edges of the cup. Tape to hold.

2 Cut eight strips from the leftover bag for the arms.

3 Draw suckers on each arm. Wrap each arm around the pencil to curl it, then slip it off.

4 Tape the arms to the inside of the cup as shown on page 107. Glue on wiggly eyes if you like, or draw eyes. Decorate your octopus with spots or rings.

Octopus Game!

One player is the "octopus" and the others are the "fish." When the octopus yells, "Swim!" all the fish move from one side of the room to the other. Any fish tagged by the octopus becomes an "arm" and helps the octopus catch the other fish as they cross the room again.

I'M A LITTLE OCTOPUS

Arm #1 goes swish, swish, swish,
(*swing arms back and forth*)
Arm #2 helps me catch fish,
(*wiggle hand back and forth*)
Arm #3 pats my head,
(*pat hand on head*)
Arm #4 makes sure I'm fed,
(*put hand to mouth*)
Arm #5 swims me to shore,
(*move arms back and forth in swimming motion*)
Arm #6 touches the ocean floor,
(*touch hand to floor*)
Arm #7 can grab and tug,
(*open and close hand*)
But all eight arms give me a hug!
(*cross arms and hug yourself*)

WHAT WOULD YOU HUG IF
YOU HAD EIGHT ARMS LIKE AN OCTOPUS?

Question & Answer

WHY DOES AN OCTOPUS HAVE INK? DOES IT WRITE LETTERS?

No, even with eight arms, octopuses don't write letters. An octopus uses the "ink" to protect itself. When it senses that danger is near, it squirts out a black inky liquid, then quickly escapes through the murky water.

Look through a clear glass of water. Now add a few drops of black tempera paint to the water. Which way is harder to see through the glass?

Giant Squid

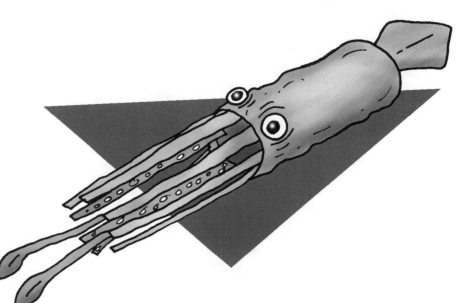

SQUID HAVE EIGHT LONG, FLOWING ARMS,
WITH TWO TENTACLES REACHING OUT.
THEY LOOK LIKE A TORPEDO
IN THE DEEP, MOVING ABOUT!

What you need

Cardboard paper tube
Orange construction paper
Tape
Child safety scissors
Wiggly eyes and glue
   (optional)
Marker

The Magic School Bus on the Ocean Floor
BY JOANNA COLE

Giant Squid: Mystery of the Deep
BY JENNIFER DUSSLING

WHAT YOU DO

1 Wrap the tube in the orange paper. Tape to hold.

2 Cut eight strips of orange paper for the squid's arms. Cut two longer strips for tentacles. Tape the arms and tentacles inside one end of the tube.

3 Cut a tail fin from the orange paper. Tape it to the other end of the tube.

4 Glue on wiggly eyes if you like, or draw on eyes. Draw suction cups on the squid's arms and tentacles.

• • • • • • • • • • • • • • • • • •

small fry FUN

Draw a squid body on paper. Glue on pieces of yarn for the eight arms and two longer tentacles. Add eyes.

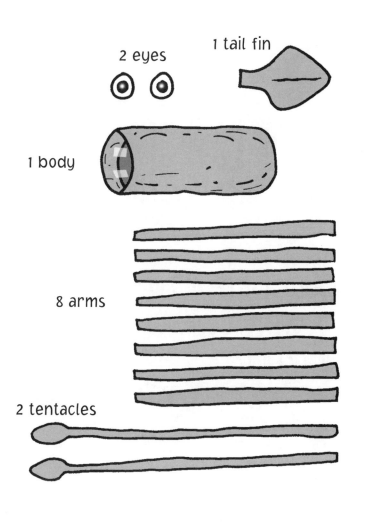

2 eyes

1 tail fin

1 body

8 arms

2 tentacles

Question & Answer

WOULD I SEE A GIANT SQUID IF I WENT SWIMMING IN THE OCEAN?

No, the giant squid lives far from where people swim. It's very hard to find and is rarely seen. Much about the giant squid is still a mystery to scientists too! Check out this web site to learn more about the giant squid: **<http://seawifs.gsfc.nasa.gov/squid.html>**

SQUID FUN!

FAMILY LOOK-ALIKES

Does a squid remind you of another animal in this chapter? If you're thinking about the octopus, you're right. A squid is a cousin to the octopus. Like the octopus, it has eight long arms. Squid are related to snails too! They're both *mollusks* — animals with soft, fleshy bodies and no backbone.

SEARCH FOR SIMILARITIES

Look at pictures of your cousins, aunts, uncles, grandparents, or other close relatives. How do you look alike? How do you look different? Ask a grown-up to help you draw your family tree. How many different people are related to you?

A SQUID SNACK?

Squid are one of the favorite foods of some whales. But the giant squid makes a really big meal — they can grow as big as a whale and can be very hard to capture! Some whales have scars on their skins from fighting with giant squid.

THE POLAR SEA

Seals and penguins
never seem to freeze.
They swim alongside icebergs
In the cold, cold seas!

Seal

What you need

Brown paper lunch bag
Glue
Child safety scissors
Brown and black construction paper
Black marker

Seals BY MARTHA E. H. RUSTAD

Sterling: The Rescue of a Baby Harbor Seal
BY SANDRA VERRILL WHITE AND MICHAEL FILISKY

fold under corners and glue down

WHAT YOU DO

1 Lay the bag flat with the flap at the top. Fold under the corners and glue them down.

2 Cut out the seal's eyes, nose, and front flippers from the paper. Glue in place. Use marker to draw whiskers and face details.

3 Put your hand in the bag for a puppet!

AWNK! AWNK!

I DON'T SEE ANY EARS ON MY PUPPET! HOW DO SEALS HEAR?

Question & Answer

Good observing! You're exactly right — true seals have no *external*, or outside, ears. They hear through small holes that have hearing parts in them, sort of like your "inner ears" that you can't see. Sea lions and fur seals are sometimes called "eared seals" because they have tiny ears on the outsides of their heads.

SEAL ACTS

PRETEND PLAY

Seals are amazing to watch! They can bend farther backward than most mammals. When they swim, their streamlined bodies *undulate* (move like a wave up and down) in the water. And some seals can hold their breath for over an hour as they dive deep underneath the ice!

TRY IT: Pretend you are a seal, crawling on your flippers. Arch your back and pull yourself forward, keeping your upper arms against your sides and your legs together. Now, pretend you are a trained seal. Practice rolling a big ball to a friend, using just your body. How did you do?

MAKE A WAVE!

Hold onto two corners of a blanket. Ask a friend to hold onto the opposite corners. Move your arms up and down at the same time to create an undulating "wave."

TAKE A BREATH

Hold your breath for a few seconds, with a grown-up timing you. Now take a big, deep breath. Unlike a seal, we need to take a breath every couple of seconds!

IN COLD AND ICE
I WADDLE ABOUT.
MY TUXEDO IS SOMETHING
I CAN'T DO WITHOUT!

Adélie Penguin

What you need

White, black and scraps of orange
  and yellow construction paper
Plastic water bottle
Tape
Glue
Child safety scissors
Wiggly eyes

WHAT YOU DO

1 Wrap white paper around the water bottle. Tape to hold.

2 Glue black paper to the back of the bottle, cutting away the bottom corners. Cut out the penguin's flippers. Tape in place.

3 Cut out a strip of black paper wide enough to fold over the top of the bottle. Fold under two corners on one end. Tape.

4 Slide the paper strip between the back of the bottle and the white paper. Fold it over the spout. Glue to the front.

5 Cut an orange beak and yellow webbed feet. Glue on the beak, feet, and wiggly eyes.

tape on flippers

glue on black paper

fold under corners and tape

glue down point

BRRRR!

Little HANDS STORY CORNER™

The Emperor's Egg BY MARTIN JENKINS

Penguin Pete BY MARCUS PFISTER

Penguins in the Fridge BY NICOLA MOON

PENGUIN FUN!

PLAY PENGUIN DAD

The male emperor penguin carries its mate's single egg on top of its feet, and protects it until it hatches — keeping the egg warm for two months or more!

TRY IT: Walk with a tennis ball or a hard-boiled egg balanced on top of your feet. How far can you get without the egg falling off?

PENGUIN CHARADES!

Penguins make sounds, but they also use certain movements to show how they are feeling. If a penguin presses its feathers down, it's announcing, "I won't bother you!" A penguin guarding a nest will stand very tall and walk slowly and stiffly, like a soldier. Penguins who like each other rub their bills together.

TRY IT: Use your body, penguin-style, to show what you want to say to a group of friends. How would you show "I'm tired!", "Let's eat!", or "Come play with me!" without saying any words?

Blue Whale

I'M THE BIGGEST CREATURE YOU'LL EVER SEE,
MY BABY SWIMS CLOSE BY TO ME.
I DON'T HAVE TEETH BUT I GET MY FILL,
MY FAVORITE FOOD IS LOTS OF KRILL.

WHO AM I?*

What you need

Blue crayon
2 white paper lunch bags
Child safety scissors
Tape
Marker
Small pieces of foil

*Answer: *The big blue whale!*

WHAT YOU DO

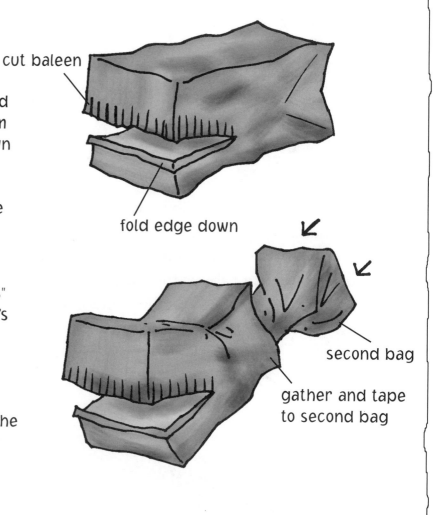

cut baleen

fold edge down

second bag

gather and tape
to second bag

1 Color both bags blue. Open one bag and rest it on its side. Cut across the bottom and along the sides of the bag as shown for the whale's jaw.

2 Fold down edges of the bag around the bottom of the jaw. Cut tiny slits around the upper edge for *baleen* (page 123).

3 Open the second bag. Gather it about 3" (7.5 cm) from the bottom for the whale's tail fin. Tape the bags together around the fin as shown on page 120.

4 Draw the whale's eyes and fins. Poke a blowhole slit and insert a foil spray in the slit as shown on page 120. Tape to hold.

small fry
FUN

Ask a grown-up to cut a long, narrow potato in half. Dip the flat side of the potato in blue tempera paint. Press onto paper for a print. Allow to dry. Use marker to draw the whale's eyes, fins, and tail.

WHY DOES A WHALE SHOOT WATER OUT THE TOP OF ITS HEAD?

A whale lives its whole life in water, but it must come to the surface to breathe air, just like other mammals, including you! When a whale surfaces to take a breath, the small blowhole on top of its head is raised above the waves. As the whale breathes out, its warm breath forms a mist in the cool air, making it look as if water is spraying out. Your warm breath does the same thing on a cold morning!

LITTLE HANDS STORY CORNER™

Rainbow Fish and the Big Blue Whale
BY MARCUS PFISTER

Big Blue Whale
BY NICOLA DAVIES

WONDERFUL WHALES

COMBING THE SEAS

Some whales have teeth, like dolphins, but some — like the blue whale — have *baleen* hanging from their upper jaws like a fringe. Baleen is made of a material like your fingernails. It acts like a comb, filtering food out of the water.

TRY IT: Use a hole punch to make lots of paper confetti. Float the confetti in a tub of water. Run a comb through the water. How much confetti did your comb pick up?

SING A WHALE SONG

Whales communicate by making clicks, whistles, grunts, or rumbles, or by singing. Some whale songs last for 30 minutes and can be heard under the water for miles (km)! Check out this website to hear whales sing: **<www.dkd.net/whales>**

TRY IT: Make up signals to talk to a friend. Use your hand to make clapping sounds or make a drumbeat on a kitchen pot or a play drum. Two loud beats could mean, "Let's go outside and play." One short beat could mean, "Time for a snack!"
Take turns making the drumbeat sound and making up signals.

WEIGHTY WHALES

The blue whale weighs more than 50 elephants, or four of the largest dinosaurs! It is the biggest animal ever known to have lived on earth! But not all whales are that big, and many don't live in the polar seas. Whales have all different shapes and names, like the humpback, the right whale, and the minke whale.

Krill

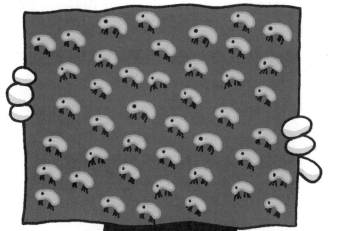

TINY KRILL GATHER IN BUNCHES,
LIKE CLOUDS IN THE SEA.
TO WHALES AND OTHER SEA CREATURES,
THEY ARE AS TASTY AS CAN BE!

What you need

White and red tempera paint, in a lid or dish
Celery stalk
Blue construction paper
Black marker

WHAT YOU DO

1 Mix the white and red paint to make pink.

2 Dip one end of the celery into the paint. Press onto the paper. Continue printing until the paper is covered with krill prints. Allow to dry.

3 Draw the krill's eyes and legs.

Question & Answer

WHY DO KRILL SWIM IN CLOUDS? I THOUGHT CLOUDS WERE IN THE SKY, AND KRILL WERE IN THE OCEAN!

When krill swim together, they make the surface of the ocean look pink, like a pink sunset! These swarms of krill are called *clouds*.

KRILL FUN!

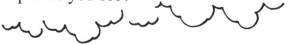

PAINT A KRILL SUNSET

Paint a sunset scene over the ocean. Dip the end of a toothpick into bright paint and make tiny dots in the ocean, like a cloud of tiny krill.

IMAGINE THIS!

Go outdoors on a sunny day when there are lots of puffy clouds in the sky. Lie down in the grass and look up at the clouds. What shapes do you see?

A

activities by skill levels
  challenging
    Adélie Penguin, 117–118
    Angelfish, 70–71
    Black Oystercatcher, 44–45
    Crab Pincers, 46–47
    Dolphin, 101–102
    Giant Clam, 72–73
    Giant Squid, 110–111
    Manatee, 48–49
    Sailfish, 98–99
    Sea Horse Scene, 32–33
    Sea-Life Mobile, 7–8
    Shark, 14–15
    Tide Scene, 52–53
  medium
    Blue Whale, 120–121
    Bony Fish Skeleton, 10–11
    Colorful Coral, 65–66
    Flat Flounder, 29–30
    Garibaldi Fish, 87–88
    Giant Kelp, 78–79
    Hermit Crab Home, 57–58
    Lantern Fish, 105
    Lettuce Sea Slug, 75–76
    Octopus, 107–108
    Porcupine Fish, 36
    Reef Fish, 23–24
    Scallop Shell, 41–42
    Seal, 114–115
    Sea Otter Mask, 82–83
    Sea Star, 60–61
    Sea Turtle Puppet, 94–95
  simple
    Amazon Leaf Fish, 27
    Brown Turban Snail, 85–86
    Jellyfish (Sea Jelly), 91–92
    Krill, 124
    My Aquarium, 18–19
    Sand Dollar Rubbing, 39–40
    Sea Anemone, 68–69
  Sea Urchin, 55–56
  toddler activities, 8, 11, 15, 19, 24, 30, 33, 56, 61, 66, 88, 92, 95, 99, 111, 121
  See also dramatic & pretend play; fingerplays & action poems; games; science investigations
algae, 80
animals. *See specific listings*
aquarium, 18–21
arts & crafts
  edible, 20, 56
  masks, 82–83
  mobiles, 7–8
  painting, 7–8, 25, 27, 39–40, 65–66, 89, 124–125
  play clay, 55, 60, 85
  puppets, 23–24, 94–95, 114–115
  puzzles, 80
  See also activities by skill levels

B

backbone, 11, 12, 92, 112
baleen, 121, 123
birds. *See* seabirds
bivalve, defined, 43
black oystercatcher, 44–45
books. *See* reading recommendations

C

cartilage, 16
clam, giant, 72–74
"clouds," of krill, 125
cold-blooded, defined, 12
coral, 65–67
crab, 38, 46–47, 57–59

D

dolphin, 6, 90, 101–103
dramatic & pretend play
  crab, walk like a, 47
  disguise, put on a, 28
  dolphin sounds, make, 102
  fish dance, 25
  play penguin dad, 119

seal acts, 116
sea urchin, 56
signal talk, whale, 123
snail crawl, 86
See also fingerplays & action poems; games

E

endangered animals, 50, 97
experiments. *See* science investigations

F

fingerplays & action poems
  fish, great big, 13
  goldfish, ocean, 87
  hermit crab, 59
  octopus, 109
  scallop, 41
  sea anemone, 68
  sea horse, 32
  sea otter, 83
  sea turtle, 96
fins, defined, 12
fish, 6, 22–37, 64, 77, 104
  characteristics of, 11, 12, 13, 22, 25–26, 34, 92
  school, 25–26
  skeleton, 10–11, 12
  types of,
    angelfish, 70–71
    flounder, 29–31
    garibaldi, 87–89
    lantern fish, 105–106
    leaf fish, 27–28
    porcupine fish, 36–37
    reef fish, 23–26
    sailfish, 90, 98–100
    sea horse, 32–35
    shark, 13, 14–17

G

games
  catch, 37, 103
  charades, penguin, 11

Crab Walk, 47
Dolphin Says, 103
Flounder Hide and Seek, 31
Go Fish, 71
Ha, Ha, 84
I Spy, 74
Same or Different?, 9
sea anemone, 69
Sea-Life Matchups, 9
tag, 106, 108
turtle (bean) count, 97
word fun, 35, 62
See also dramatic & pretend play; fingerplays
    & action poems
gills, defined, 12

H
habitat
    cereal-box exhibits, 21
    defined, 20, 80
    hunt, 21
    puzzle, 80
    types of, 21
        coral reef, 64–76
        deep sea, 104–112
        kelp forest, 77–89
        open sea, 90–103
        polar sea, 113–125
        sandy shore, 38–50
        tide pool, 51–63
hermit crab, 57–59

J
jellyfish. *See* sea jelly

K
kelp, giant, 77, 78–80
krill, 124–125

M
mammals, defined, 50, 84. *See also* dolphin;
    manatee; seal; sea otter; whale

manatee, 48–50
mollusk, 42, 112

O
octopus, 6, 107–109, 112

P
penguin, 113, 117–119
plants, ocean, 6. *See also* algae; kelp

R
rafts, defined, 84
reading recommendations, 9, 12, 17, 21, 26, 30, 34,
    40, 46, 52, 57, 61, 66, 72, 79, 82, 85,
    87, 91, 94, 107, 110, 114, 118, 122
recipes
    play clay, 55
    slime, 76
reptile, defined, 96

S
sand dollar, 39–40
scales, fish, defined, 12
scallop, 41–43
school, fish, defined, 25
science investigations
    backbone, 11, 12
    balancing, penguin egg, 119
    "baleen" filtering, 123
    birdcalls, 45
    camouflage, 28
    collection, start a, 43
    communicate with signals, 123
    compare & contrast, 9, 11, 13, 16, 31, 34, 35,
        43, 63, 67, 43, 47, 58, 59, 80, 81, 86, 93, 112
    endangered species, 97
    flotation, 16, 93
    growth, 31, 67, 80, 81
    light, 106
    movement, 35, 43, 56, 86, 93, 100
    octopus "ink," 109
    sea "jelly," squishiness of, 93

senses, 16, 97
shapes, 100, 125
shell, 43, 74
size sort, 81
sounds, 26, 35, 102
spines, of porcupine fish, 37
suction power, sea star, 63
tide pool changes, 54
wave motion, 116
sea anemone, 64, 68–69
seabirds, 6, 38, 44–45
sea horse, 32–37
sea jelly, 6, 90, 91–93
seal, 113, 114–116
sea otter, 82–84
sea slug, 75–76
sea snail, 85–86
sea star, 60–63
sea turtle, 6, 90, 94–95
sea urchin, 55–56
seaweed. *See* kelp
shark, 13, 14–17
shells, 38, 41–43, 74
skill levels. *See* activities by skill levels
snout, 34
spiny-skinned animals, 40, 62
squid, giant, 104, 110–112
starfish. *See* sea star
swim bladder, in fish, 12, 16

T
tide, defined, 53
tide pools, 51–63

V
vertebrae, defined, 11

W
websites, 17, 20, 50, 67, 112, 123
whale, 6, 112, 120–123
word play, 35, 62

MORE GOOD BOOKS FROM WILLIAMSON PUBLISHING